EDUCATION 3 TO 5: A TEACHERS' HANDBOOK

MARION DOWLING

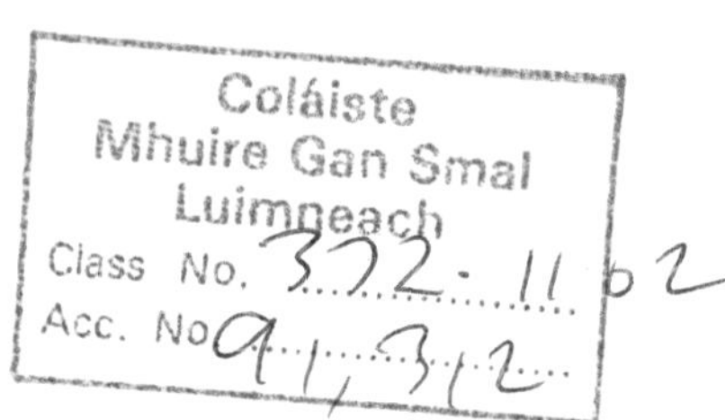

First published 1988

Paul Chapman Publishing Ltd

British Library Cataloguing in Publication Data
Dowling, Marion
Education 3 to 5: a teacher's handbook.
1. Education, Preschool
I. Title
372′.21 LB1140.2

ISBN 1 85396 002 0

Typeset by Katerprint Typesetting Services, Oxford
Printed and bound by Butler & Tanner Ltd, Frome and London

CONTENTS

PREFACE AND ACKNOWLEDGEMENTS

Nursery practitioners and trainers continue to voice concern about the lack of professional books available to support their work. Research texts are available, many revealing fascinating insights into how young children learn. There remains a gap between theory and practice, however, with the increase in research findings and more pressures on teachers, this gap is widening. In times of stress people continue doing what they know they do best; innovation can be threatening.

Many teachers are open to dynamic practice, but time for study remains a problem. How can they read educational theory when the practicalities of the next day loom ahead? Theory often proves to be taxing reading; the teacher cannot be expected to concentrate on material which initially seems to be mentally inaccessible at the end of a busy working day. Yet any practitioner fortunate enough to have the opportunity for full-time study will be the first to enthuse about the joy of having time to read, reflect and discuss reading with colleagues.

This book is intended for the practising nursery teacher. In considering some major research findings, the author attempts to make the bridge to the nursery classroom. Chapters 5 and 6 focus on the teacher's own evaluation and professional growth to support her work. Chapters may be read independently, and sections dipped into.

References and sources will be found at the end of each chapter. Sections focusing on 'suggested action' occur regularly throughout the text.

For the sake of convenience only, the teacher is referred to as 'she' and the child as 'he'.

My gratitude to Terry, my husband, for his patient and practical help.

INTRODUCTION

In December 1972 the White Paper *A Framework for Expansion*[1] proposed that within ten years nursery education would be made available to those children of three and four years whose parents wished them to benefit from it. This proposal followed recommendations by the Plowden Committee,[2] which estimated that provision would be required for 90 per cent of four-year-olds and 50 per cent of three-year-olds in England and Wales.

The fourteen years following the White Paper have proved an interesting mix of depressing regression and exciting development. The promised national wide-scale expansion of nursery education never took place. In a period of general contraction, provision for the non-statutory age range is particularly vulnerable. Some local education authorities have closed down their nurseries; others have built units and have been unable to equip and staff them for the under-fives. Of particular concern are the authorities which have made an effort to provide a school placement for nursery-age children but lack the necessary resources to support an appropriate curriculum or organization. If we do not include this latter group of children, who cannot be said to be receiving a nursery education, the spread of provision throughout the country is very thin. In 1976 capital expenditure for nursery education stood at £46 million. In succeeding years it fell to less than £15 million. Part-time and full-time nursery places in England were available in 1980 to a mere 19.7 per cent of the population, as estimated by Plowden.

On the other hand, research projects relating to the under-fives have been considerable. Studies have shown the crucial nature of the early years with regard to growth and development. John Brierley's work on the rapid development of the brain in the young child is particularly impressive in stressing the importance of an early favourable environment.[3] Concern about the piecemeal development of care and education for the under-fives led in 1977 to a Schools Council project on 'continuity of experience'[4] and to an associated project on 'transition and continuity in early education'.[5] The effectiveness of different pre-school programmes has been studied, and varied work has focused on how children learn and the central role that parents play in their child's development and learning.

Perhaps most important, long-term studies have revealed that early education can offer children identifiable long-term benefits. The High Scope pre-school curriculum began in Ypsilanti, Michigan, in 1960, when people in the United States were starting to think seriously about how to help 'disadvantaged' children. In a long-term study of this project, David Weikart, the main instigator, claims that this methodology is sound in offering pre-school gains. He argues that money invested in a child's earliest education can show returns for society in terms of less expenditure on later remedial education, less expense containing delinquent behaviour and increased future employment prospects for the participants.[6]

This US study is supported by findings from the Bristol longitudinal study of a cohort of 1,400 children born in one week in April 1970. Seventy per cent of these children from a range of social backgrounds experienced at least three months in a playgroup, nursery school or day nursery. At the age of five and again at ten these children's performance in reading, maths and general intelligence tests compared favourably with the 30 per cent of the group who had not received such experiences.[7]

It is also useful to consider the relative benefits of different forms of provision. A study by Jowett and Sylva observed two matched groups of forty-five children with playgroup and nursery experience on entry to infant school and in their third term at school. The groups were carefully matched for age, sex, parental occupation, birth order and housing. Children were also observed in a wide variety of activities. Results of the observations indicated that those with nursery experience were more autonomous, determined and persistent in behaviour and that these traits continued during the first year at school.[8]

The current picture, though patchy, is one of growth. Supported by project findings, local authorities are cautiously developing their early education programmes through support offered to the voluntary sector as well as by means of state provision. Exploratory courses have developed, with emphasis on multi-professional co-ordination and training for those working with the under-fives. In some areas the High Scope approach is being piloted and evaluated. Some authorities are supporting low-cost provision using a combination of professional and parental skills; yet others are using spare infant classrooms to develop a nursery programme. For some areas of the country, particularly the inner cities, there has been no contraction but a continued expansion under Inner City and Urban Aid programmes involving many exciting examples of co-operation between statutory and voluntary agencies.

A great deal of confusion remains over the different provisions for children under five. The variety is tremendous. At four a child may attend a reception class in a main school, a nursery-school class or a combined family or nursery centre. He may have a place in an industrial private day nursery or a local authority day nursery, or he may go to a playgroup or a private school or be placed with a childminder. These provisions have their own distinct purposes and functions, and are financed, staffed and organized differently.

Such diversity makes any common training unlikely at present. However, at the OECD Conference in Paris in 1980 recommendations were made which would apply to any satisfactory policy for young children.[9] These included flexible and varied provision, decentralization to enable parents and children to participate and no imposition on parents and children to opt for one 'best' type of provision.

It is unrealistic to aim to provide a book which will embrace such diversity. Rather, I have attempted to make a statement about quality education and care for children aged three to five years. The justification for any educational resources to be offered to children under five is to facilitate cognitive development. This can be effective only if intellectual growth is considered alongside the total development of the child and the very close links that each child has with his family. Many provisions pay attention to the child's learning process – but this may be in a context where priority is placed more on adult education and the quality of parenting, as in many playgroups, or on offering the child from a less favoured home a stable daily environment, as in day nurseries. In an educational establishment, whether nursery class, school or family centre, the ideologies and training of staff focus on the child learning. This demands a sound knowledge of child development and early childhood curriculum on the part of the adult, with acknowledgement of the interdependence of any learning and development at this stage. If we are looking at educational provision for young children, the case for the professional nursery teacher is a strong one. It becomes even stronger if we consider the young child with special needs. Here a measure of early and appropriate intervention can assist in preventing educational failure and avoiding the need for expensive and less effective remedies at a later stage.

In this book I hope to clarify and support the best of these educational practices. I refer to the nursery and the nursery teacher, in the knowledge that many other adults, particularly nursery assistants, are involved in many of these practices, and it is hoped that they too will find the book relevant.

The finance available for nursery provision is extremely varied. Equipment and premises are likely to vary tremendously from a community playgroup to a social services day nursery to a nursery classroom to an infant classroom. While purpose-built, well-equipped buildings are helpful, these are not the nub of nursery education. The essential resources are skilful and sensitive adults working to provide for the children. It is not productive to put forward a polarized view for either voluntary or statutory provision. At present we need to maintain all that we have and to make sure that it is as good as it can be. However, if local education authorities do have additional resources, priority should surely go to training and employing nursery teachers who maintain a model of practice themselves but who work closely with the other providing agencies.

The term 'pre-school child' is convenient but negative and not in any way descriptive of the exciting stages of development that occur during these early years. References to 'rising fives' or 'under-fives' are similarly unhelpful and can be positively insulting if we are seriously considering the capabilities and needs of a three- or four-year-old. Accepting a need for shorthand, however, the child from three to five is referred to in this book as 'the young child', and those under three are termed 'toddlers'.

The increasing involvement and interest shown by central government in curriculum development have affected all phases of education. Because it is non-statutory, the nursery sector is not included in the range of curriculum discussion documents recently published. Nevertheless, if we consider nursery education as an integral part of the education system, there must be debate and discussion about the purposes and practices of this stage of education. The author firmly believes that developing young children's learning is complex and demanding. It is recognized that teachers need help in clarifying their ideologies and support with the practicalities of the work. Consideration of this nursery practice includes the care and pedagogy that we offer to young children, how we offer them and how we can check that we are being successful in our practices.

REFERENCES

1 Department of Education and Science (DES), *Education: A Framework for Expansion*, HMSO, London, 1972a.

2 Central Advisory Committee for Education, *Children and Their Primary Schools* (The Plowden Report), HMSO, London, 1967.

3 J. Brierley, *A Human Birthright: Giving the Young Brain a Chance*, British Association for Early Childhood Education, London, 1984.

4 S. Cleave, S. Jowett and M. Bate, *And So to School*, National Foundation for Education and Research NFER/Nelson, Slough, 1977.

5 P. Blatchford, S. Battle and J. Mays, *The First Transition: Home to Pre-School*, NFER/Nelson, Slough, 1982.

6 C. Breedlove and J. Schweinhart, *The Cost Effectiveness of High-Quality Early Childhood Programmes*, High Scope Educational Research Foundation, Ypsilanti, Mich., 1982; report prepared for the 1982 US Southern Governors' Conference.

7 A. F. Osborn and J. E. Milbank, *The Association of Preschool Educational Experiences with Subsequent Ability, Attainment and Behaviour*, University of Bristol Department of Child Health, 1985; report to the Department of Education and Science.

8 S. Jowett and K. Sylva, 'Does kind of pre-school matter?', *Educational Research*, Vol. 28, No. 1, February 1986, pp. 21–31.

9 Conference of the Organisation for Economic Cooperation and Development (March 1980). Report from the Director of the Centre for Educational Research and Innovation.

1

THE CONTEXT OF CURRICULUM PLANNING

Throughout this book constant reference is made to different aspects of children's development, together with suggestions as to how best to foster this development. The danger of such an approach is that, by separating these aspects, the interrelationship of growth, development and learning tends to be forgotten. Let us therefore start with a pen portrait of the whole child.

Sean is four years old. He can play sociably with other children on most occasions, although sometimes he finds it difficult to share and take his turn in play activities. He relates well to other adults but at times of stress or uncertainty clings to his mum. Sean is able to feed, wash and dress himself but has difficulty doing up his shirt buttons and cannot yet tie his shoelaces. He is now able to run, skip and hop and is starting to keep time to music. Sean particularly enjoys playing outside and engaging in lively pretend play with others. He also likes to paint and make models; however, although these activities are often tackled with vigour initially, Sean soon tires of them and if given the opportunity will rush off from the painting area to another occupation. Sean finds life full and interesting. He laughs and talks a lot both to himself and to his friends. His use of language includes suggesting ideas for play, describing his past experiences and giving a running commentary on his own activities. When talking Sean often pauses as if searching for a word to describe his feelings or thoughts. When things go wrong and friends cross him Sean's language deserts him, and he is likely to punch and kick to maintain his rights.

Sean or his equivalent is familiar to every nursery teacher. The teacher's task is to ensure that Sean's time in the nursery is worthwhile. What is worthwhile is in itself open to debate, but the statement of the aims of education found in the Warnock Report is surely very acceptable, namely: first, to enlarge a child's knowledge, experience and imaginative understanding, and thus his awareness of moral values and capacity for enjoyment; and secondly, to enable him to enter the world after formal education is over as an active participant in society and a responsible contributor to it.[1]

To start to achieve these aims for Sean and other children in the nursery the teacher must plan a curriculum. Sean's curriculum needs to take account of his abilities, interests and weaknesses. Any offered curriculum includes the environmental setting – the experiences and messages that children receive in school. Yet what the teacher believes she is offering may not be what is being received by the child. The *received* curriculum depends entirely on what children take up, and this in turn depends on how the curriculum is offered.

Effective curriculum planning involves (1) a knowledge of how young children develop and learn most effectively, (2) familiarity with the materials, activities and methods that promote different types of development and learning and (3) the resources available in terms of time, staff numbers and expertise, accommodation and equipment. Although this planning will affect what happens in the nursery, the child's learning has already started in the home and will continue after nursery hours. The power of home influences and the way parents can be a key resource for their children also deserve careful study.

These aspects are considered in subsequent chapters. However, apart from the immediate factors to consider, such as the children's needs and the resources available to support learning, there are more general influences in today's society. We need to consider these to gain some picture of the complex environment in which many young families are living.

YOUNG FAMILIES

The younger the child, the more inextricably he is involved with his family. Thus, some consideration of current family structures is relevant. The conventional family unit consisting of a married man who is working with wife at home and two dependent children accounts for a mere 5 per cent of households in Britain today. The range of family patterns varies tremendously. While marriage remains popular, one in three marriages is likely to end in divorce, and over 60 per cent of divorces involve children under sixteen. Teenage marriages are particularly vulnerable. Young couples in late adolescence enter into a partnership with unrealistic expectations, and the problems of sharing a life together can be greatly worsened with the arrival of a young baby; often there are not the resources to deal with a demanding young child.

Young children may also come from one-parent families, from a partnership where parents are cohabiting or from step-families where one parent has remarried. Although most children under four years still live with two natural parents, it may be assumed that marital disharmony exists in many of these households before the break-up of the partnership.[2]

The position of women is seen to have changed. Widening educational, social and work opportunities have encouraged them to expect the same things in life as men. Potentially they have a bewildering number of choices. Some groups urge them to gain satisfaction from child rearing and the home; others urge them to find fulfilling jobs and to expect shared parenting from their partners. This last expectation is often not met. The fashion is to talk of role reversal and sharing the upbringing of children; but studies indicate that, although fathers' involvement with their families has increased, the majority still place their work first and families second.[3] Even women who work full time still see their families as their first responsibility.

Unemployment is widespread throughout Britain, but certain regions are particularly affected. Workers in low-paid, unskilled manual jobs are in particular danger of losing their jobs and remaining unemployed for long periods.[4] Children of all ages are likely to be affected by their parents' loss of income and of self-esteem. The youngest children, being at home more of the time, will be especially exposed to some of the associated effects, such as an increase in family violence and child abuse.

Even without unemployment, there is a vast inequality between standards of living. There is still no minimum wage. In 1982 the relative earnings of the lowest-paid men were lower than at any time during the 1970s.[5]

Many young families in both urban and rural areas live in inadequate, overcrowded housing with little play space. The National Children's Bureau Child Development Study[6] found that by the age of sixteen one in five children had lived in a home which lacked the basic amenities of bathroom, hot water supply and indoor lavatory. Present reductions in current expenditure suggest that these families are not likely to benefit from any increase in Welfare State support.

Thus, certain parents have a particularly demanding job in child rearing. There are also influences which affect all strata of society, and one of particular concern is the increasing number of reported cases of child sexual abuse. It is estimated that at least one in ten adults was sexually assaulted during childhood. Child molesters are usually successful in concealing their behaviour, and although work is developing with offenders the majority continue to repeat the offence.[7] This highlights the need to help children to be frank with adults and to seek protection at the youngest age. If nursery teachers are involved with the total development of the child they must share with parents some responsibility for this area.

TECHNOLOGICAL DEVELOPMENTS

Home life for young children has been greatly affected by technological developments. Children under five watch a lot of television. In 1973 children starting school in Norfolk were able to name, unaided, sixty-nine television programmes they had enjoyed – this without their being able to read.[8] This survey took place at a time when pre-school programmes were just being introduced on television, and a later report from a study of 165 children under five showed that pre-school programmes were more popular, although advertisements were watched most of all.[9] It may be that as television has become more established very young children watch it less. In 1972 it was estimated from parental interviews that young children watched between twenty-three and thirty-three hours' television a week. In the 1984 study home observations revealed that on average young children watched for sixty minutes a day. Parents may have overestimated their child's viewing time by assuming that, if a programme was on, it was being watched. In the 1984 study, television sets were on and available to children for between approximately three and a half and four and a half hours daily – a far greater time than the children spent consciously watching.

These figures may perhaps temper the belief that many young children do nothing at home but watch television all day. Tizard found that young children are involved and interested in all aspects of home life – 'the neighbours, money, electric lights, the structure and arrangement of homes, parents' work, God, the death of pets, doctors'.[10] However, the fact that television may prove to be a common home experience for many children at some time in the day can be useful. Television is potentially good second-hand experience for learning, if used with discretion. Both studies quoted found that parents do not spend much time viewing with their children; yet, as with most activities, adult intervention and interest could increase stimulation for the child. We should also remember the stages of conceptual development in order not to overestimate what young children can understand from moving pictures. How can the relative size of an elephant be portrayed to a three-year-old on a screen? The ability to listen, concentrate and complete a task is an essential learning skill, and the amount of background noise and television on offer for young children to take or leave may affect the development of this skill.

There has been no study yet of the effects of home computers on this age group. We know, however, that young children have ready access to these as well as to sophisticated electronic toys. As a result they are likely to develop a facility and knowledge of this equipment which we cannot afford to ignore. Both television and computer programmes provide young children with lively stimulus that can affect early reading skills through aiding visual discrimination and sound/symbol correlation. If we are to build on home experiences and complement rather than substitute for what the home offers, then these indicators about how young children spend their time at home are significant.

PARENTAL INVOLVEMENT AND MINORITY GROUPS

One major educational issue which is continuing to affect teachers, parents and children is the notion of parental involvement. Although this notion is currently fashionable and still regarded by some practitioners as an innovation, it was considered an integral part of nursery provision as viewed by Margaret McMillan when she opened her nursery school in Deptford in 1911. She claimed that the nursery school, although available to all children, should be the special right of the working class parent:

> And the working class mother, what of her nursery? To begin with it would seem much more important to make her sovereign, if not ruler of this new domain, rather than to assume at once that she can never be anything but an outsider. . . . The existing nursery schools are not yet controlled by the mothers of the children who attend them. But already parents' committees are being formed.
>
> Already, too, it is clear to many that the nurseries must be built as an annexe to homes and that as far as possible the homes should open on to these child gardens so as to make the frequent visits and constant oversight of mothers a possibility.[11]

Margaret McMillan speaking today would be at the forefront of current thinking. Many of her plans were at the time too advanced to be considered, and it was not until the Plowden Report in the 1960s advocated a partnership with parents that these ideas regained some cautious support. Support and developments in this area have continued, albeit in a piecemeal way, for the past twenty years, receiving official government approval in the White Paper *Better Schools*.[12] Despite this the notion is a complex one; the term 'involvement' means many things to different people. Later in this book we examine the findings of recent research studies, with suggestions as to how a nursery can develop profitable relationships with parents that will be beneficial to all concerned.

The nursery teacher today works in a climate which encourages parents to become more informed about and active in their child's education. The media provide a range of books, magazines and radio and television programmes specifically for young parents. The pre-school playgroup movement must be admired for its energy and enthusiasm. Many parents concerned with this movement have learned a great deal about their young child's development and how they can promote it. Other parents may have read widely and taken every opportunity to make the task of parenting enjoyable and positive. These parents will assist their child's confidence and provide an interested and enriched home environment, which every teacher knows is the right background to enable children to take advantage of a nursery experience.

Other parents are interested in their child's early education but may be misinformed. Tizard's two-year intervention study, which tried out different ways of involving parents in nursery classes and schools, revealed that there are large gaps in some parents' understanding. Despite intensive efforts from nursery teachers, many parents remained unclear about the purposes of nursery education, and parents from ethnic-minority groups were particularly keen to have reading and writing skills developed from the earliest age.[13]

A further group of parents may not see the relevance of their role to their child's development. Van der Eyken's study of Home Start in Leicester reveals an approach to working with isolated, depressed and hard-to-reach families.[14] The criteria for the success of this scheme are increased confidence of the parent, reduction in family stress and reduction in children at risk, rather than any consideration of early childhood education programmes. Admittedly these three groupings are crude – parents are individuals, and any programme of involvement must consider individual needs and attitudes. However, it is a good starting-point to consider the concluding comments in the DES study *The Young Child at Home*:

> We cannot emphasize strongly enough the love, pride and interest that all the parents in the sample showed towards their chldren. Nursery staff have a unique opportunity to establish relations with parents at the initial stages of a child's

school career, to capitalize on this goodwill and boost the parents' own sense of responsibility and confidence in their ability to contribute to their own children's education.[15]

Apart from influences in the home, other changes in society are reflected through recent research reports and subsequent legislation. Different ethnic and cultural backgrounds are an important influence on how children are reared and educated. There are now about three million immigrants and their descendants in Britain today. While some of these people have been assimilated, others have remained culturally distinct. The Swann Report on minority groups made a strong bid for a pluralistic approach to society – for all to acknowledge the diversity of race, colour and creed which exists in many parts of the country but to appreciate the contributions that each distinct group can offer.[16] Racial tensions nevertheless exist, and young children who live with prejudice will learn through imitation. Studies have indicated that attitudes are forming by the age of three. Thus, the onus is on any educator of young children to provide a model of tolerance based on interest in and understanding of differences in people. In areas which are not yet multi-ethnic in composition the need is perhaps even greater to prepare children in our nurseries for future living in a pluralistic society.

Apart from the need to develop sound attitudes in the nursery the teacher has the task of accommodating children of ethnic minorities and providing for those who are either unable to speak any English or without sufficient control of English as a second language. In these circumstances it is often very difficult for practitioners to judge the level of functioning of these children. Skilful assessment is required to identify particular gifts and abilities as well as any need for special help, apart from language development.

SPECIAL NEEDS

The increasing concern over early identification and support for children with special needs has been heightened with the Warnock Committee's recommendations and subsequently the 1981 Education Act. The concept of 'special educational needs' was introduced embracing those children with mild learning difficulties or with minor emotional or behavioural disorders, as well as those with more obvious handicaps. A child with a major disability is likely to have been assessed previously and then placed in a nursery with additional support from appropriate agencies. Conversely, the child whose special educational needs are included in the broader view is much more likely to be admitted to a nursery before any assessment has been made. This places a particular responsibility on the nursery teacher to identify any sign of special problems or needs at the earliest opportunity.

It is impossible to separate assessment from continuing care and education of the child. In all cases of special needs the nursery teacher is responsible for devising individual learning programmes which are regularly monitored. These programmes will be effective only if they are developed as a result of knowledge of early development and of how the handicapping condition affects it. Warnock stresses that

> although we see parents as being the main educators of children, whenever possible we recognize that many parents will be unable to bear this responsibility without help and we therefore recommend that reinforcement and skills should be provided for parents of children with disabilities or significant difficulties in the earliest years.[17]

Some local authorities have particular resources to do this in the form of home visiting schemes such as the Portege Project of specialist peripatetic teachers. Parents may also be supported through voluntary organizations or self-help groups. Nevertheless, the parent who has a child with special educational needs placed in a nursery will look to the nursery staff for a regular source of advice and help.

Thus, the implications for working profitably with a range of children with special needs are many. Warnock recommends that the integration of all special needs, including a child with serious disabilities, 'may be of inestimable value in helping to increase his self-confidence and pave the way for his successful integration into an ordinary primary school'.[18] However, the increased work-load and its complex nature should not be underestimated when considering the in-service needs of nursery staff and the learning needs of other children in the nursery.

EQUAL OPPORTUNITIES

The changing role of women and the move for men to take a more active role in family care has already been mentioned. If we believe that early learning experiences can and do affect subsequent achievement and the development of attitudes in later life, it is essential that all children are offered as far as possible equal learning opportunities and that former rigid role expectations are reassessed more broadly. The nursery teacher has a special responsibility to ensure that these learning experiences are not affected by difference. The Equal Opportunities Commission suggests that 'stereotyping can blind a teacher or a parent to the individual talent and potential of a girl or boy, and by restricting the expectations of the adult, stereotyping can severely restrict the aspirations of children to their detriment in adult life.'[19]

Traditional nursery provision has encouraged girls to be immersed in home play and boys to be engaged in construction activities. Many books for young children still reflect mothers at home and fathers involved in outside work; girls are often shown as dependent and kind and boys as more assertive and lively. In today's nursery the adult needs to be sensitive to how her provision, organization and attitudes affect the way young children view their own role and that of the opposite sex. By offering children a full range of activities the nursery teacher can then observe what children select. This selection will usually reveal their preferences and strengths. The teacher's task is to help broaden their experience. Having clarified this, parents will need to be made aware of these issues and as far as possible encouraged to support non-stereotyping in their own homes.

THE EDUCATIONAL CLIMATE

The general educational climate has changed in recent years. What effects is this likely to have had on the education of under-fives?

After the exuberant expansion and optimism of the 1960s, the 1970s brought a period of contraction to education. Nurseries were the first to suffer from falling rolls. From 1974 to 1979 the total number of qualified teachers in nursery and primary schools in England and Wales had fallen by approximately 3,000 to 194,000.[20] This sharp fall was not clearly foreseen, and nurseries along with primary schools were consequently placed in the stressful situation of having to find sufficient numbers of children to protect the continuing employment of staff. Contraction in schools coincided with economic recession, and the entire education service was regarded critically in terms of its effectiveness. Public funds were not readily available for innovation. Even without cuts in capital and revenue expenditure, inflation often meant that schools had less spending power. Thus, with effectively fewer resources schools were under close scrutiny to see what they could achieve with children.

Accompanying this was an increased movement toward teachers and the education service in general being made accountable to society. The interest in monitoring procedures was reflected in setting up the Assessment of Performance Unit, which aimed to follow and judge children's standards of performance over a period of time. While some local authorities undertook to concentrate on children's attainments, others focused on developing self-appraisal schemes for their teachers and schools. All approaches were aiming toward a closer and more controlled look at classroom procedures and outcomes.

The nursery teacher, although involved in non-statutory provision, is nevertheless affected by these developments. Her task is complicated by the fact that nursery pedagogy is in the main process-based and difficult to assess in hard terms. Moreover, as a result of contraction nursery teacher training was cut back heavily. In the courses that remained, the early retirement of nursery trainers and failure to replace them meant a worrying loss of expertise. We currently face a general increase in the number of young children entering school, and many local authorities are hard pressed to find staff to appoint who are qualified in this phase of education.

These developments provide a backcloth for any nursery establishment in the country. If the job of educating and caring for young children is to be sensitively tackled, all these influences are relevant to planning, and some of the practical implications are discussed later in the book. Considered in this way, the complexity of the work becomes apparent; a balanced attitude is essential for any nursery practitioner, bearing in mind that whatever is current or fashionable, the children's developmental needs are all-important.

In recent years we have learnt a great deal about different aspects of child development, some of which will be explored later. Kelmer Pringle's fourfold description of children's needs, in her book *The Needs of Children*, remains sound. Dr Pringle claimed that all children require (1) love and security, (2) praise and recognition, (3) new experiences and (4) responsibility. This provides a good starting-point for any debate on curriculum.[21]

Suggested action

The child in the family

- Consider how much useful and relevant information you have about the home background of each child in the nursery. What additional information do you need?
- Review the procedures that you have for acquiring background information about children. How can these be improved? For example, through contact with parents; through formal and informal links with other agencies.
- Select those children who you consider to be adversely affected by

family circumstances. List the ways in which these adverse effects are manifested in behaviour.

- List the ways in which your provision is helping to meet these children's needs: (1) through curriculum provision; (2) at specific times of the day through procedures and routines; (3) through particular attention from an adult.

Effects of sexual abuse

- Be aware of changes in behaviour. Timidity, over-anxiety and inappropriate sexual approaches by the child to adults may possibly be caused by abuse. Take considered action; if you have real concern on the basis of close observation and objective evidence you should discuss the matter with your headteacher, the family health visitor or social worker. Your concern regarding the child's behaviour needs to be shared with the parent at an early stage.
- Be aware of the sensitivity of this topic in the nursery. Meet with small groups of parents to raise the issue of helping children to protect themselves from an early age, and discuss any approaches before you use them.
- Help children to recognize what is a wrong touch or embrace. Use dolls or puppets to role-play and demonstrate private parts of their bodies.
- Help children in a worrying situation to trust and tell an adult. Offer many examples through stories, and discuss with children the need to have one grown-up to confide in.

Effects of the media

- Consider how much you know about the television and radio programmes available for young children. How important is it for you to increase your information?
- Note the number of comments from children arising from their viewing television programmes and how the viewing is reflected in their play.
- Consider how often you use these occasions to develop active learning; e.g. to create a familiar television puppet character and use this for developing conversation with children. Make a relief map layout of a scene in a favourite programme, with pipecleaner figures, for miniature role-play.
- Design a simple illustrated guide for parents, offering advice on the most constructive use of television programmes with their children at home.

- Invite parents to the nursery for an informal meeting to share their views on children's television programmes, and offer them this guide.

Growing up in a multi-ethnic society

- Check how much you know about the life-style and culture of children from different ethnic groups attending your nursery. What sources are available to you to learn more?
- If you work in areas which are not yet multi-ethnic in composition, consider how you can prepare your children for living in this society. Useful influences can include books, jigsaws, photographs, magazines and videos; e.g. using magazines, suggest that a small group of children identify and cut out all the different faces they can find – this can promote valuable discussion; introduce an ethnic doll into the home corner.
- Check the relative value that is given to mother tongue and dialects in the nursery. Different languages should be shared and given equal status. For example 'How do you say "thank you" to your mummy at home, Indu?'
- Identify the children from minority groups in the nursery, including traveller children, as well as different religious, cultural and racial groups. Assess how you are promoting the self-image of these children by encouraging them to share information about their background. For example, collections of items brought in from home to add to interest tables; sharing in celebrations of ethnic and minority-group festivals; learning simple songs from different cultures.
- Encourage the development of social relationships across cultural and ethnic groups by grouping certain children together at different times and encouraging collaborative tasks.

Equal opportunities

- Consider your own attitudes relating to sex stereotyping and share these in staff discussion with colleagues.
- Look at the apparatus and the way it is used in the nursery, noting the messages conveyed to children in terms of sex stereotyping.
- Consider the stories that are offered and the way family roles are represented. Aim to offer a balanced view of family life through literature; e.g. the sharing of working life in and outside the home by both partners.
- Listen to your conversations with children and note where you are

encouraging individuals to develop a restrictive role image. For example, 'Big boys don't cry'; 'Little girls don't shout like that – try to be a lady.'

- Aim to offer stories and incidents from your own life as a model; e.g. 'Mr Smith cooked the tea last night while I did the ironing.'

Children with special needs

- Consider the balance of children in the nursery and identify those who have special needs according to the Warnock definition.
- Consider two of these children with special needs:
  - How much joint information do you have about the present learning capabilities of each child?
  - What additional information do you need about the handicapping condition affecting the learning?
  - How comprehensive and effective is the individual learning programme you have devised for each child?
  - How can you achieve more?

The educational climate

- Discuss how the present educational climate of contraction and accountability has adversely affected morale and inhibited developments in your nursery. Has it also led to more constructive and purposeful work with children and their families?
- Consider how you can justify the different provisions you make for young children.
- Plan in your staff group for each member in turn to take an aspect of the nursery curriculum and analyse the effect it can have on children's development and learning. These 'presentations' can later be offered to groups of parents.

REFERENCES

1 Department of Education and Science (DES), *Special Educational Needs: Report of the Committee of Enquiry into the Education of Handicapped Children and Young People, under the chairmanship of Mrs H. M. Warnock*, HMSO, London, 1978.

2 J. Haskey, 'Marital status before marriage and age at marriage: their influence on the chance of divorce', *Population Trends*, Vol. 32, 1983, pp. 4–14.

3 N. Beail, 'The role of the father during pregnancy and birth', in N. Beail and J.

McGuire (eds.), *Fathers: Psychological Perspectives*, Junction Books, London, 1982. L. McKee, 'Fathers' participation in infant care: a critique', in L. McKee and M. O'Brien (eds.), *The Father Figure*, Tavistock, London, 1982.
4 L. Rimmer and J. Popay, *Employment Trends and the Family*, Study Commission on the Family, London, 1982.
5 Department of Employment, *New Earnings Survey*, HMSO, London, 1982.
6 M. Fogelman (ed.), *Britain's Sixteen Year Olds*, National Children's Bureau, London, 1976.
7 M. Elliott, *Preventing Child Sexual Assault*, Bedford Square Press, London, 1985.
8 G. Dunn, 'Television and young children', *Early Childhood*, Vol. 11, No. 2, 1981, p. 11.
9 C. E. Davie, S. J. Hutt, E. Vincent and M. Mason, *The Young Child at Home*, National Foundation for Educational Research/Nelson, Slough, 1984.
10 B. Tizard and M. Hughes, *Young Children Learning*, Fontana, London, 1984.
11 M. McMillan, *The Nursery School*, Dent, London, 1919.
12 DES, *Better Schools*, HMSO, London, 1985.
13 B. Tizard, J. Mortimore and B. Burchell, *Involving Parents in Nursery and Infant Schools*, Grant McIntyre, London, 1981.
14 W. Van Der Eyken, *Home Start: A Four Year Evaluation*, Leicester Home Start Consultancy, 1982.
15 Davie *et al.*, op. cit. (note 9).
16 DES, *Education for All: Report of the Committee of Enquiry into the Education of Children from Ethnic Minority Groups, under the chairmanship of Lord Swann*, HMSO, London, 1985.
17 DES, op. cit. (note 1).
18 Ibid.
19 Equal Opportunities Commission, *An Equal Start*, EOC, Manchester, 1982.
20 DES, *Statistical Bulletin 17/79*, HMSO, London, 1979.
21 K. Pringle, *The Needs of Children*, Hutchinson, London, 1974.

2

CURRICULUM PRINCIPLES INTO PRACTICE

In pioneering nursery education early in the twentieth century, the McMillan sisters and Maria Montessori were working at a time of tremendous social disadvantage, with children who were ill-fed, poorly clothed and badly housed. The accent was on social rescue, and this played a part in nursery pedagogy for some years. Respect, care and a range of play activities were offered to young children, together with a heavy emphasis on good hygiene and daily routines. Susan Isaacs,[1,2] working in the Malting House School, built on these practices and added the very clear message that provision was not sufficient in itself and that the adult's role is crucial in developing the child's learning. Detailed and sensitive observations produced evidence of children thriving on these practices, and today's nursery practice still remains rooted in these early approaches. However, there is today a need for an even closer scrutiny of practice to ensure that nursery education is recognized and valued.

In 1974 Barbara Tizard described the nursery curriculum as 'essentially one of free play supplemented by music and stories'. This curriculum, she said, can hardly be distinguished from that of the home; and the children 'are taught at home and at school by very similar methods'.[3] Strong support is offered later in the book for parents and nursery personnel to work together in the closest partnership. However, such attempts to blur any difference between the home and an establishment funded and staffed to develop and nurture young children can only undermine the latter's professional status.

The onus is on the nursery teacher to retain the good aspects of traditional practice but to set these within a clear framework of thinking for her work. A purposeful rigour with the accent on extending children intellectually is required to justify provision. The public increasingly wants to know what children are learning in a nursery, rather than being satisfied with the provision of a place of social care and safety. Nursery practice must therefore be based on principles which have developed from the increased research and knowledge now available about the nature of learning and the needs of young children.

Today's nursery teacher will develop her principles as the pegs on which to hang her practice. No principle, however fine, is any good unless it can be directly translated into classroom action. Conversely, the teacher should be able to look at her curriculum content and the way she organizes her teaching and link all this to her educational principles. Theory and practice need to go hand in hand.

It is also necessary to be strictly honest when linking practices and principles. Are some routines adhered to because they promote children's learning or because they are convenient for the adults managing children? Are some messy activities withdrawn half-way through a nursery session because it is in the interests of children to limit curriculum choices at this stage, or because the adults find it easier to clear these up before the lunch hour? Providing an honest reason for all nursery activity can be a painful exercise, but is necessary in clarifying the purposes of provision. This chapter is concerned with identifying some key principles which might be taken as a basis for planning a nursery curriculum.

THE CHILD AS INDIVIDUAL

In every child genetic endowment and environment have combined to make him unique and special. Because young children are relatively unsocialized and because of their limited experience and egocentric stage of development their individual characteristics will be particularly noticeable. Every nursery teacher knows this and will also accept that, while the pattern of growth and development follows a universal sequence, the rate and progress of this development differ for each child.

It is the child's developmental stage that is significant for his learning, rather than his chronological age. The wide variation in developmental stage can affect all aspects of a child's growth. It may relate to his understanding of concepts, to his gross or fine motor control and to his social and emotional level of development. What are the implications of this knowledge for the nursery teacher? John Brierley states that

> The important point is that each child is born unique because of 'nature's gifts' and he or she needs a unique environment to maximize them. It follows from

> this that in the home and at school it is *just* to treat different children differently as long as each is treated as well as possible. Blanket treatment is no good.[4]

If children are individuals, each will possess his own particular route to learning. It is the skill of the teacher to identify that route, to discover exactly how she can help that child to be motivated to learn.

As well as regarding learning needs, the teacher must be aware of the individual's personal, social and physical requirements. Children differ in their personal make-up; the transition that they make to school is partly determined by their approach to change and their ability to adapt to a new situation. The nursery teacher, in acknowledging differing needs, must offer support where it is most needed. She has to recognize that not all children are willing or able to join in a large ring game, for example, and must provide a quiet table activity as an alternative. Not all children in the nursery wish to absorb themselves with messy activities, and such preferences should be respected when voiced by a child as they would be if they came from an adult. A wide choice of activities needs to be available to provide for all tastes. Some children revel in boisterous outside play which challenges physical skills; others are cautious and tentative in their efforts to master body skills. It must be accepted that some children prefer to stay inside rather than face the elements, and within reason and the constraints of practical circumstances this choice should be available.

Physical needs are also individual. If drinks are provided for a mid-morning break, children will vary in their ability to consume a standard amount. Likewise, despite the desirability of developing 'good habits', individual bladder capacity and sphincter control do not make it sensible for children to go to the lavatory at set times.

Every nursery teacher, then, needs regularly to ask herself how her acceptance of children as individuals is reflected in her practice. This is not to say that the entire nursery programme will be geared to responding on an individual basis at all times. One of the processes of maturation is for the child to become socialized, but this process needs to be tackled sensitively and at the appropriate developmental stage.

If children are truly seen as individuals, every one can be regarded as having 'special needs'. Many handicapping conditions involve developmental delays in one or more aspects of growth. This delay must be identified by the teacher with specialist help, but the child will require the same rich nursery provision with the opportunity to operate at the appropriate level of development reached. Thus, the five-year-old who has a developmental delay of two years in intellectual ability is likely to be playing with concrete materials of clay, water and sand, exploring them through the senses. The five-year-old whose development is two years ahead may still be using these materials but will be beginning to represent his experiences in many abstract ways.

Every child's uniqueness and the ways in which he is best able to flourish in a nursery setting need to be answered by the teacher at the earliest possible opportunity.

Suggested action

Determining principles

Each member of staff should list ten curriculum principles relating to nursery practice, each principle to be copied on a small card. All cards are then shuffled and distributed equally among the group. A large sheet of paper should be prepared as indicated (Figure 1). Each member of staff is required to read out the principle on one of her cards in turn and indicate in which column she wishes to place it. She is required to justify her decision to the group. All cards should be placed in this way. The aim of the activity is to allow no more than ten statements in either the 'essential' or 'important' columns, and this will be achieved through clarification of terms and negotiation within the group.

Essential	Important	Unimportant

Figure 1

Meeting individual needs

- Select a child at random and write down all you know about him as an individual. Identify how you attempt to meet his particular needs by a programme of activities/adjustment of routines/your behaviour towards him.
- Consider how you meet children's individual needs during story time; e.g. introducing stories ranging in length and content; ensuring a group of children of manageable size and identifying those who can still receive a story only on an individual basis; varying the approach to reading and telling stories through using puppets, sound effects, dramatic voice; focusing on particular stories which match children's own situations.
- Mark each child's cloakroom peg with his photograph (this can be a photograph requested from home or one taken on admission to the nursery).
- Set up an obstacle course for children which gives scope for them to crawl through a tunnel, balance along planks, jump and climb. Carefully observe individual children's reactions to this activity. Which of them refuse to attempt the course? Who is willing to try with support and encouragement? Who is confident and competent? Who becomes very competitive?
- Provide a range of materials in painting, sticking and cookery areas to encourage children to exercise individual choice when producing something of their own.
- Ensure that you gain an accurate total picture of each child through close observation. For example, a child who has particular ability in one area of development may be expected to have good all-round development; the child from a poor social background with behavioural difficulties may be expected to achieve less than he is able.

NURSERY PROVISION AND THE TOTAL EDUCATIONAL PROCESS

Sound learning should be based on what is already known and should move cautiously and gently toward the unknown. Learning is best fostered when there is sufficient challenge to stimulate and interest but not so much that too dramatic an adjustment is required. This is particularly important with young children, whose experience is necessarily limited and who are even less equipped to make jumps in their learning.

In the past there have been remarkable discontinuities in our school system. Nurseries considered themselves to be something special and apart. Parents were respected and there were some links, but despite Margaret McMillan's own philosophy there was little acknowledgement of the power of the home environment. Nurseries were cut off from the rest of the school system, largely because of their own modest, complacent and insular attitudes. Within the infant school, teachers tended to be autonomous; they had their own children and their own approach to the curriculum, using their own resources which were firmly kept in their own cupboards. Children were often subjected to totally different approaches to learning, and it is a tribute to the resilience of some that they ended up literate and numerate.

In recent years a tremendous amount has happened as a result of the growing awareness of the need to promote continuity of experience at all levels of learning. Although for the teacher the first transition in which she is involved is the child's move to the nursery, in fact it may be far from the first move for the child – he can arrive in a nursery from a variety of placements. Possible transitions experienced before transfer to a nursery are:

(1) Home to nursery.
(2) Home to playgroup to nursery.
(3) Home to childminder to nursery.
(4) Home to childminder to playgroup to nursery.

Clearly the regimes and messages offered to children in these different placements will affect the nature of the move to the nursery. The nursery, unlike other phases of education, accepts children who have not shared a previous common experience. In coping with this diversity of background and personality the nursery teacher has a particularly challenging job. The NFER study on *The First Transition* from home to nursery found that in the main the children who had come from high-scoring backgrounds (enabling, warm, loving homes) tended to relate better to other children, were found less in solitary and unoccupied activities in free play and showed less lost or negative behaviour in a directed session such as story or register time.[5] These findings reinforce the tremendous difference between those best prepared and those least prepared to enter a nursery class.

There is no doubt that all children have had a fund of experience before they come to school and have learned a great deal in their own way. It is essential that each child is accepted from where he is. It is not enough to allow the learning to continue in the rather random and *ad hoc* way that it has to date – it is certainly not satisfactory to ignore what has happened before. The emphasis must be on a planned intervention based on previous learning.

A child has to learn a tremendous amount when he moves from home to school. Mary Willes indicates the range of language skills that has to be acquired:

> In taking on his new role of pupil, the newcomer to school has to be put to the test of using the language learned in interaction at home. He has to find, or to extend his resources to include, the language of a learner, one among many, in an institutionalized setting. He has to wait his turn, and recognize it when it comes, to compete, to assert his rights and sometimes to give ground. He has, in short, to discover what the rules of classroom interaction and behaviour are, what sort of priority obtains among them, and how and when and with what consequences they can be broken.[6]

Some children will attune to these requirements smoothly and easily; for others they will constitute a major stumbling-block. Until the young child adapts fully to his first transition there is no doubt that his learning will be arrested or will take a backward step.

When looking at the entry to nursery, a general pattern emerged from the NFER study. The experience was that quite close attention was paid to the child and his family initially. Phased visits to the nursery were planned, with encouragement for parents to be involved. Once the child had appeared to settle, however, the study describes his two worlds as 'slipping apart'. Parents were interested in their child's nursery experiences, but they were very wary of doing at home anything deemed unacceptable by the school; because they hesitated to request more information about what happened during the nursery sessions, they remained uninformed. The research team said that it interviewed too many parents who had no more information about their child's progress than 'he's happy' or 'getting along satisfactorily'. A fair amount of work was undertaken by nurseries to involve parents, but there were often not enough individual requests to parents for them to do specific tasks. The study also highlighted a lack of liaison between playgroups and nurseries. Little information was received from playgroups when children entered the nursery, and a number of nursery staff were unaware of what experiences had been offered in the previous setting.[7]

The other major transition involving the child and the nursery teacher is the move to mainstream school. In many ways this transition can prove even more traumatic if insensitively handled; the move involves adapting to a class which does not have a nursery staffing and may lack the space and play resources of a nursery.

In the knowledge that under-fives may be accommodated in so many different types of provision deemed 'nursery', the adjustment to be made in the main school will vary according to circumstances. However, the following areas relating to a move may cause young children anxiety:

(1) The school building – in particular a vast stretch of playground, long corridors, large lavatory blocks and the complexity of building layout.
(2) Daily routines – most vulnerable times for young children are the daily transitions: moving into the hall, being in the playground, changing for PE and lunchtimes. These times are most overwhelming when large groups of children are involved.
(3) The learning experience – in the nursery the most usual procedure is for children to have unlimited choice of available activities while adults supervise or become involved with small groups. In infant classes the most prevalent mode is for children to be engaged in prescribed activities while the teacher is either actively engaged with the class as a whole or working with a group. The transition into main school usually means a restriction of choice for the child.
(4) The ratio of adults – a further NFER study observed that many young children reacted to being in large groups with few adults in the following ways:

    (a) impatience at having to wait for the teacher's attention;
    (b) covering the ears to shut out noise;
    (c) bewilderment and dismay in mass situations;
    (d) failure to respond to instructions given *en masse*;
    (e) inability to keep still and quiet for sustained periods;
    (f) unwillingness to pool creative work.[8]

There is in addition the need to ensure continuity of experience for young children within the nursery. Does the nursery team ensure that there is consistency in handling children? Are the expected standards of behaviour, noise and tidying up common to all? A consistent approach to common situations needs to be agreed. For instance, how do we react to a child who insists on taking every painting and model home with him? There should be opportunities for continuous activities from one day to another; can the nursery teacher ensure that a construction of bricks can be left to be completed the next day?

All nursery teachers work on different aspects of liaison and continuity within and between schools. The question remains of how much more can be achieved. Regarding the transitions to and from the nursery, teachers should ask themselves how much they know about what any one child has experienced before he becomes a nursery pupil, and how much they know about what he is going to experience after he leaves the nursery.

Suggested action

Find out about the child's home background

There is no single successful strategy for acquiring relevant information about the child's home background, but the following approaches are likely to be useful for different catchment areas.

- An initial home visit offering an invitation card for the child to start at the nursery. Home visits remain controversial, and in practice some teachers are more highly motivated and more suited to the job than others. However, there is no doubt that some parents are more at ease on their own territory when meeting their child's teacher for the first time – and this can equally apply to the child.
- There should be an opportunity in school or at home for the parent to talk to an interested adult about the unique characteristics of her child. Some parents may respond very well to completing detailed questionnaires, while others will find it easier to chat. Whatever the approach the emphasis should be on communicating positive traits rather than just potential problems.
- A range of occasions for social, fund-raising and curriculum purposes can encourage teachers and parents to meet and can foster trusting relationships (see Chapter 3).

Find out about previous playgroup experience

Previous attendance at a playgroup may indicate experience of a small-home group offering security but mainly sedentary activity, or the other extreme of a large group accommodated in a hall with adults providing few boundaries for learning and socialization – with a range of other provisions in between. The teacher's knowledge of this experience can be extremely useful. Good established relationships with playgroups can ease communication.

- Aim to visit playgroups in your catchment area each term to build up a picture of their style of management and expectations of children.

- Invite playgroups to visit the nursery in session; use opportunities to discuss different styles of working with children.

Check you have sufficient information

Select three children at random who have entered the nursery during the last term. Make a list of all you know about each child's previous learning and relevant home experience. Make a note of any additional information you would like to enable you to work more effectively with these children. Consider appropriate strategies for gaining this information; e.g. home visits with the aim of asking parents specific questions about their children; invitations to individual parents to visit the nursery and talk generally about their child.

Observe children during their first week in the nursery

- How do they leave their parents at the start of the session?
- How do they settle to activities?
- How do they relate to other children and adults?
- How do they greet their parents at the end of the day?

Plan for individual need

- The child who finds transition to the nursery difficult may require: (1) parents to stay with him until he has settled; (2) flexibility in attendance, gradually building up to a daily attendance; (3) substitute parent attached to the child during initial sessions (this role could be given to a volunteer parent or National Nursery Examination Board (NNEB) student).
- The child who finds it difficult to relate to other children may need: (1) the initial security of one adult; (2) gradual introduction to work on a specific task with one other child, with adult present; (3) withdrawal of the adult as he gains confidence.
- The non-English-speaking child will be helped by the initial presence of parent or volunteer helper who is bilingual, and by early involvement in repetitious rhymes and jingles and familiarization with regular routines with associated labels, e.g. 'wash your hands', 'time for lunch'; introduction to one or two socially responsible children who will involve the child in play.

Aim for a smooth transition from nursery to main school

- Both nursery and infant teachers must learn to appreciate each other's work in meeting the developmental needs of the children. This can be facilitated by nursery teachers leading main-staff in-service sessions focusing on nursery practice and by infant teachers joining nursery staff discussions. Occasions should be available for joint discussion of children. Regular exchange visits and exchange of nursery and infant posts will enable a better understanding of each other's age group.

- Compare the information about your children that you wish to pass on to the infant teacher with the information she requires. Consider carefully where there is a mismatch and why.
- Where a nursery class is attached to a school, any curriculum policies must be developed with the nursery as the starting-point.
- Continuity of experience should be developed through daily routines. The entry to school in the morning, procedures for playtimes, gathering for story time and collecting and returning resources – these routines can be eased for the child entering the main school if an attempt has been made to follow the procedures previously established in the nursery. Discuss your daily programme with your infant colleague and compare and contrast your routines, your expectations of children and your priorities during the day.
- Foster continuity of experience by deliberately duplicating pieces of equipment used in the nursery for the child to recognize in the infant classroom. A favourite teddy found in the home corner, or familiar books, can be reassuring to the less confident child when he is settling into his new placement.
- Encourage the infant teacher to use additional adults to help children with unfamiliar routines. Parents can be very helpful during the initial move into the infant classroom: during undressing and dressing for PE; helping children to adapt to lunchtime procedures, including mealtime supervision in small groups; involvement with supervisory assistants in organizing small group games after lunch.
- Use the opportunities offered by an attached nursery unit to allow older children with developmental delay to spend some time back in the nursery and younger able children occasionally to join appropriate sessions in the reception class.

LEARNING THROUGH ACTION AND TALK

Young children learn most effectively through their actions and through talk. They will continue to learn without entering a nursery – the power of the home environment has already been mentioned – but the nursery teacher should clarify the particular sort of experience she can offer which will nurture learning.

Young children are very ready to please and learn certain things through imitation. It is possible through regular practice and repetition for a group of four-year-olds to recite a numerical table or recognize a number of flashcards. While this 'performance' may impress a lay person it is highly likely that only an image of learning is being seen, with children incapable of making sense of the symbols or of being able to apply their knowledge. In such cases the learners have been required to receive certain information to regurgitate at a later date. No independent learning has taken place.

How do young children learn best? Piaget's main findings remain as valid as ever, even if some aspects of his work are increasingly challenged. Young children gain information through having active encounters with their world, and they process this information into theories and assumptions which form their mental structures. These structures are in turn extended and amended in the light of new information being gathered and fed into what already exists.[9]

John Brierley suggests that 'Through exploration, play and speech the young brain seems to strengthen. A child needs this two-way dynamic relationship with the environment.'[10] Ausabel supports this view, arguing that, although discovery learning and problem-solving are relatively complex forms of learning, they are the most effective means of intellectual functioning for the young child. Received learning through symbols and verbally presented concepts, although simple in cognitive terms, will come only at a later stage of maturity.[11] Thus, a three-year-old may competently sort out household items in the home corner, classifying and matching. He is not yet able, however, to make sense of the code of arithmetic (see page 45).

Having offered the case for young children to learn through concrete experiences, it may be helpful to consider the different roles of exploration, play and talk in development. In exploration the concern is with finding out about reality. Corinne Hutt's study of play and exploration illustrates that exploration precedes play; her sample of nursery-aged children were given a novel box for the first time:

> When a child had thoroughly explored the novel object, he then sometimes used it in symbolic play, for example by pretending it was a bridge or a seat. It was only when the child had apparently learned all there was to know about the object that it was incorporated in play activities, and any further learning was purely incidental.[12]

Thus, through exploration the young child gains information from an experience and modifies or accommodates his learning accordingly.

There is a tacit acceptance among educators that play is a useful educational method to promote in a nursery. However, a distinction must be made between closely structured, target-oriented activity and unstructured, child-initiated play. There is a place for both approaches in a nursery programme, but the teacher needs to be clear about their respective benefits.

While highly structured play has a clear purpose, and exploration leaves the child more open to discover what he will from materials and apparatus, they are similar in that the aim is for the child to find out something new and modify his experience accordingly. In highly structured play, apparatus is used for a specific purpose, giving little space for the child's creative thought. The Montessori approach is a good example of children tackling activities in a way prescribed by the adult. This may be valid as part of a learning programme designed for an individual child, but it is limited as a general diet for children.

Conversely, child-initiated, spontaneous play is open. This approach allows the child to engage freely in pleasurable activity and thus to consolidate skills, actions and meanings previously acquired through exploration. Spontaneous play allows the child to take his knowledge of the real world and try to make sense of it. He will assimilate this play into his framework of experience, but it requires less modification or accommodation, since his activity is based on practising or representing what he already knows.

The most obvious example of this is in pretend play. Vygotsky has in mind this play, which he considers important for young children because it frees them from the constraints they constantly meet in real life; in a world of all-powerful adults the four-year-old can escape to become master of his world through play.[13] Vygotsky sees play as necessarily involving the creation of an imaginary situation, and Joan Tamburrini suggests that his work creates a link between spontaneous play and the development of imagination at a later stage. The young child creates a situation but needs concrete props to represent different objects and settings. As he matures he is able to relinquish these props and to create meanings and situations through mental activity.[14]

It can be argued, then, that opportunities for exploration and for structured and unstructured play all have a place in the nursery. Sylva, Roy and Painter considered the educational value of play and defined complex play as an activity which is goal-oriented, whether the goals are imposed by adult or child. For them the important consideration was that the child felt he had accomplished something. They also looked for evidence that the child in his play is able to link a series of actions and engage in long-range planning and organization of his behaviour. Play was also regarded as complex where an object or act was seen to represent something else – that is, through symbolic or pretend play. These authors also considered the child's concentration span; where there was evidence of absorption and resistance to distraction the task was rated as more intellectually demanding.[15]

Turning to John Brierley's third requirement, a great deal has been written on the significance and structure of language. Suffice it to say that it provides a powerful means for personal development, for reflecting on experiences and for communicating thoughts to others. How this facility is developed has been hotly debated. In 1965 Chomsky put forward a strongly supported notion that the child possesses a 'language acquisition device' which enables him to absorb scraps of conversation and discourse, and through this sensitive mechanism he can make out grammatical rules and thus build up a framework of knowledge.[16] While this was more than acceptable at the time, with the benefit of further investigation the emphasis turned from the view that language was acquired as something accelerated and apart from other aspects of development; interest turned to the whole child and his range of experiences. John Macnamara suggested in 1972 that language develops precisely because the child uses all his previous knowledge and experience to make sense of a situation.[17]

Margaret Donaldson offers the following example:

> An English woman is in the company of an Arab woman and her two children, a boy of seven and a little girl of thirteen months who is just beginning to walk but is afraid to take more than a few steps without help. The English woman speaks no Arabic, the Arab woman and her son speak no English. The little girl walks to the English woman and back to her mother. Then she turns as if to start off in the direction of the English woman once again. But the latter now smiles, points to the boy and says: 'Walk to your brother this time.' At once the boy, understanding the situation though he understands not a word of the language, holds out his arm. The baby smiles, changes direction and walks to her brother. Like the older child she appears to have understood the situation perfectly.[18]

Donaldson stresses that as far as the two children were concerned both were in a position to understand the intentions of the group; the meaning of words was extracted from the behaviour of the people. Thus, language learning is now seen to be very closely tied up with other aspects of development. The child must be placed in a position where he can understand what is happening – which will depend on what has happened to him before and how he has accommodated and assimilated these experiences.

Emphasis thus falls on the child as an active learner. He is required to make links between events and behaviours and then to draw his own conclusions. In so doing the child discovers that language represents these events and behaviours.

The next stage is one of practice and consolidation; developing linguistic skills are used in a range of contexts with other people. In the nursery the child learns according to his stage of development to use and practise language for the purposes outlined by Joan Tough.[19] He will use it to maintain and promote his interests and well-being, and then as a vehicle for developing his thinking – to examine a range of possible solutions to problems, to predict, hypothesize and plan. As he learns to use talk for these purposes, language gradually becomes detached from immediate experience. The emphasis has so far been on the particular effects of exploration, play and language on children's learning. The practitioner, hopefully convinced of these key ingredients, now needs to reflect on how she can plan to include them.

Any richly resourced nursery environment provides a range of opportunities for exploration. The traditional provisions of sand, water, clay, dough, paint and blocks will all initially be explored by the young child, leading to his discoveries of their various properties. Dry sand is usually explored first with the hands. The child may poke, press and trickle it and bury his hands in a heap of sand. He may delight in the cold, heavy feel of the sand and let the fine grains tickle his skin. Clay is not visually attractive and it requires to be touched to discover its capabilities. The cold, clammy nature of clay may repel some children until they meet the challenge of prodding and pushing it to change its shape. Natural potter's clay is most satisfactory for the young child. The intention is to provide not a modelling material but something to work with and explore. Exploration can be staged and guided through provision. Clay should initially be offered to children without water or tools; harder lumps of clay can then be presented with a bowl of water. The child is able to change the substance from something unmalleable to an oozing semi-liquid. The further addition of blunt knives, clean lolly-sticks and pieces of cut-off broom handle will then allow children to explore clay with equipment.

As we have seen with sand and clay the young child's explorations will be through his senses. He needs to see, listen, taste, touch and smell his environment until he is ready to accommodate to these experiences.

In structured play, planning will play a large part, because some outcomes are predetermined for the child. In extreme forms of structured play apparatus is required to be used for one purpose only, and any other uses are discouraged. An inset jigsaw is an example of structured apparatus. The teacher who is determined to channel the learning along her lines will gently dissuade the child from using the inset pieces to stand up and represent animals and people – she regards the task of completing the jigsaw as the aim. Unstructured apparatus may also be used for structured play. Blocks may be provided with a request for children to build a car. The teacher may return to the group on a number of occasions to check that all the car body parts are being assembled. There is thus restricted space for children's creativity in this task, although there is value in seeing how the group tackles the activity and in observing who emerges as a leader.

Provision of an extreme form of unstructured play requires the adult to be present but passive. Practitioners who subscribe to this approach have no clear ideas how they can promote children's cognitive development through play. They tend to concentrate on the therapeutic value of the activity. Almy suggests that a symptom of their preoccupation with the emotional is apparent lack of involvement in the intellectual life of the child.[20] Tizard states that in nursery schools where teachers adopted this passive role the play was generally of short duration and poorly elaborated.[21]

Where symbolic play is recognized as valuable in promoting children's learning, the teacher needs to take a more active role. This play is increasingly valued for helping consolidation skills and meanings, aiding imaginative development and revealing language structures. The teacher can structure the environment by arranging a setting for an imaginative play area or by limiting the range of blocks available; by actively observing the level of play she can also obtain diagnostic information.

The teacher may also choose to be involved in children's self-initiated play by playing alongside and offering a reassuring presence, by questioning, suggesting or providing additional props. The 'daddy' who has hurt his leg at work will be better able to play out his role with the addition of a bandage and a walking-stick. The adult needs to be aware of the potential for learning in children's play, but this is a different matter from predetermining the play. The teacher may have set up a structure in her provision for home play with graded sizes of saucepans and lids. She must accept, however, that the child is not necessarily going to seize on this graded equipment and develop an understanding of relative size. The play may be purely imaginative, with the purpose of getting the meal cooked and served on the table. If this is so then intrusion would be counter-productive. If, however, the teacher observed the child selecting a wrong size of lid which he tries to fit on to the saucepan, it may be appropriate to suggest trying an alternative and to observe the fruits of this in future play.

The teacher should also be influenced by research findings pointing to the most profitable areas of play. Sylva saw the most challenging and complex play in child-initiated music, small-scale construction, art (where the child selects his own medium), large-scale construction and structured materials such as jigsaws. Here she observed children working with care, using imagination, planning in a systematic way, learning a skill and working towards a goal. However, she admits a further necessary dimension to worthwhile play, that of 'sustained commitment': 'The ability to manage one's own attention is a prerequisite to effective and satisfying social relations. And of course the ability to concentrate is crucial to later school work.' Pretend play scores highly on this dimension. While it is regarded as an activity of only moderate cognitive challenge, children were found to be absorbed, and this play was seen, together with miniature play and sand and water activity, as a means of encouraging children's talk. Sylva suggests that these activities may be more relaxed and less goal-oriented, thus providing an easy setting for conversation.[22]

A somewhat gloomy picture of the nursery as nurturing ground for young children's spoken language is offered to us by recent research. Thomas observed a small group of children for a day and managed to record every utterance from them and from the adults. She found that the teachers were prepared to accept minimal comments from children and that their own exchanges with children rarely helped to develop discourse or thinking skills.[23] In the Oxford Pre-School Research Study, Woods reports that 'incidence of really interesting talk is rare',[24] and Sylva supports this in her study: 'Its finding suggests that the pre-school is not an ideal environment for teaching children the many skills of conversation, since coherent conversations are few and far between.'[25] Tizard's studies, too, indicate that children's speech at home is likely to be richer than in a day nursery or nursery school.[26] Tizard refers to the 'puzzling mind' and 'persistent curiosity' of the four-year-old and suggests that the individual attention and intimate setting of home are more likely to satisfy these needs.[27]

We need to look critically at these findings. In both the Oxford studies mixed samples of playgroups and nurseries were used. Tizard's 1975 work was based on day nurseries, and the 1984 research used a sample of only thirty four-year-old girls. It is valid to ask in this latter case just how far the findings can be related to other children. The research nevertheless does offer some clear messages to nursery teachers, who can only benefit from comparing their own practice with these findings.

Although the adult's role in promoting conversation has been emphasized, there is much to be said for encouraging children to talk together. Clark, Robson and Browning indicated that peer-group settings often provided opportunities for children to play with words and to initiate conversations in a way that does not happen with an adult present. Peer groups can also be helpful to children with more limited language and to those from non-English-speaking backgrounds. In these cases it has been found that children will help others to pronounce words and understand meanings.[28]

The nursery environment itself can influence talk. Sylva observed some of the richest dialogue in home corners or dens where an enclosed, intimate space had been created. She also noted that there were more instances of children conversing with one another in nursery rather than playgroup settings. Sylva recommends that teachers review their programmes and materials to encourage children to interact in pairs.[29] Pairing of children was seen to have potential for challenging play as well as for dialogue. The teacher's specific role in promoting talk is discussed in Chapter 4. If she is to be convinced of the importance of this work and to feel relaxed in giving time to it she must be supported by her headteacher, parents and policy-makers. Katz refers to 'the institutional imperative which presses teachers to "cover" the curriculum and prepare their pupils for "the next life"'. She suggests that where teachers are under such pressures to develop academic skills, the communication skills which aid intellectual growth will not be nurtured.[30] Bearing in mind that infant teachers have great difficulty in nurturing communication skills with large groups of children, the nursery should act as a 'bridge' between home and school.

The Bristol Language Development Study of 1972–81 focused on children's talk in the home as well as their spoken language development in the transition to school. Although the role of the nursery is not considered, the study has implications for nursery teachers. MacLure and French found that some similar language strategies were employed in the home and at school, such as 'pseudo-questions' where a request for information is made to which the questioner already has the answer. Differences were nevertheless found in that in the home children were likely to question the adult but this was rare in school. Children's spoken language is corrected both in school and at home, but the study found that while the child might correct the parent at home it was very uncommon to find the teacher corrected by a child in a reception class in school. The authors conclude that the school setting may, if anything, present the child with a more limited set of conversational options than he has become familiar with at home:

> Just as the child at home has more latitude to ask questions and evaluate and correct his adult interlocutor, so also he has more opportunity to introduce new topics and to attempt to change the topic of conversation . . . Such opportunities are much less frequently available to children in school, firstly because much of the talk is done for pedagogical purposes . . . and secondly because of the complexities involved in handling conversation involving large numbers of participants.[31]

The nursery is surely in the ideal position to ease this transition and to provide plentiful opportunities for the type of talk that already occurs at home, at the same time guiding some conversation into pedagogical channels.

Suggested action

Exploration

- Check that all activity areas have provision for exploring materials in a variety of ways. For example, painting and sticking: cardboard boxes of different sizes, stapler, polystyrene shapes, corks, pipe-cleaners, feathers, wool, paint, glue, sticky tape, fabrics; home corner: variety of kitchen implements, flour sieves, beaters, whiskers, equipment to 'mend' including a large box of spare parts from washing-machines, typewriters, radios and vacuum-cleaners, with tools for mending; outside area: mud patch with digging implements and encouragement to use hands to find as many treasures as you can; 'bicycle maintenance shop' with spare parts, cycle pumps, spanners and cleaning equipment; large construction corner with ropes, wooden boxes and planks, plastic milk crates, barrels and blown-up tractor inner tube.
- Introduce an interesting artefact, e.g. muscial box, by placing it without comment in the home area and observe the way individual children find out about it. Note how their approach alters according to the stage of development of each child.

Structured play

- Consider how much of your apparatus and materials has a defined use for the child; e.g. some fitting and grading apparatus, jigsaws, miniature dolls with specific dressing-up outfits.
- Assess when these materials are particularly useful; e.g. in helping a child acquire and practise a specific skill.
- Consider how you as a teacher structure children's play:
  - through your provision and by setting up situations;
  - by requiring that apparatus is used in a particular way; e.g. Lego is for building and not to be used as pretend food in the home corner;
  - through time, e.g. the allotted time for children to become involved in inside and outside play;

- through determining use of space; e.g. a very small home corner may allow only one or two children to play freely;
- through your own involvement in the play; e.g. taking a role, initiating actions and suggesting actions for the children, linking one child with another in play.

- Consider how much of this structure inhibits or enriches children's play. This will depend on particular circumstances and particular children.

Spontaneous play

- Observe a child's spontaneous play and note how often he initiates action, through suggestions or his own activity; how often he leads; how often he follows; how long he sustains the play; his use of talk to extend and enrich the play.
- Use this observation as a means of planning curricular opportunities for specific children; e.g. the 'dominant' child to work in a collaborative activity with other strong personalities; the child who 'flits' to be encouraged to sustain his involvement in other situations.

Talk

- Move around the various activity areas to determine the most fruitful activities for promoting talk; e.g. large-scale, boisterous play is unlikely to give children time to use language as a tool for thinking, although they may need briefly to communicate with one another.
- Focus on productive areas for play as indicated in research studies, e.g. clay, sand, water, construction and home play. Spend some time in each of these activities listening to the quality of conversation.
- Identify those children who help to foster conversations in groups. Aim to 'use' those children in other situations to assist their peers.
- Set up situations which require children of different linguistic abilities to communicate and collaborate; e.g. two children to mix the dough and colour it with paint, to sort out painting aprons and identify those that need mending, to lay out the drinks at break time.
- Help children to develop social conventions with one another, e.g. waiting to enter a discussion and listening to another point of view.
- Carefully observe children with limited English-language skills.

Learn to interpret the basics of their first language, their body language or, if the child is deaf, any utterances. Help these children feel secure in knowing that you understand their needs and will help them attach appropriate words to express their needs.

EARLY MATHEMATICIANS

We have seen how young children start to accommodate to new experiences through spontaneous play and associative language. At the same time these experiences allow them to detect patterns and relationships; they begin to see similarities and differences, to notice how things are ordered, fit together and correspond. This early mathematical awareness is yet another way young children have of making sense of their world. As with other aspects of learning, the mathematics is embedded in experiences, and related language is gradually learned. The nursery teacher needs to check that the child's words express true comprehension:

> A facility with mathematical language does not necessarily mean that understanding is present, nor will children learn merely by being presented with words. On the other hand, first-hand experiences are so important that children who have had opportunities to handle and manipulate real things may have considerable mathematical understanding, although they may not necessarily have the linguistic labels to attach to their knowledge. This emphasizes the importance of teachers observing children's actions very closely as well as listening to their language when assessing the level of mathematical understanding.[32]

The teacher must recognize the main elements that constitute early mathematical development and realize the potential for learning in everyday nursery activities and routines. These elements are as follows.

Spatial awareness

The child's earliest experiences are concerned with space: positions in space and shape. Having had opportunities to move around in different spaces, to handle objects of different shapes and sizes and to fit them into spaces, arranging and rearranging things, the child learns about distance. In so doing he builds up some understanding of terms like 'near' and 'far', 'in between' and 'behind'. However, it is necessary to be aware of the young child's thinking at this stage. This thinking is quite consistent but influenced by particular events. Piaget's work indicated that children's beliefs about proximity are at this stage influenced by the presence or absence of barriers. For instance, the art easel may be judged to be near to the window; if the distance remains the same but a table is placed between the two, the child will consider that the art easel is now further away from the window. Perception of distance is also influenced by the amount of effort and time going into an activity. To the young child, climbing up a steep hill is further than running down it.

Through increasing knowledge of their own body, young children learn different ways of fitting in and moving in space. Most will not yet understand the invariance of space; they cannot accept that a large ball of clay remains the same even when it is broken into small pieces. They are also only just starting to distinguish two-dimensional from three-dimensional shapes, and Piaget's studies indicate that at this stage young children are not yet ready to appreciate another spatial viewpoint. Recent research has challenged this, however, showing that under certain conditions the child's spatial understanding is considerably more mature (see page 62).

The beginnings of measurement

For young children to learn how to measure accurately they need a range of experiences in making judgements about amounts. The experiences should be with weight, length, distance, time, area and capacity and should lead to the use of such words as 'heavy', 'light', 'long', 'short', 'near', 'far', 'today', 'yesterday', 'wide', 'narrow', 'full' and 'empty'. Such early judgements tend to be crude and inaccurate, but it is important to accept them as the child's own and through further experience and discussion to enable him to refine his views. Early judgements are made through comparisons. This happens through children handling materials and conversing with one another, suggesting who has more or less milk or who has collected bigger stones. Children need to judge how much paper or material they require to cover a surface, and the teacher may join in at this stage to ask if the amount is too much or too little.

Early judgements about time and speed may be helped by stopping and starting at a given signal from the teacher and comparing time intervals during the course of activities. At this stage of thinking a young child is likely to confuse the type of task he accomplishes with the length of time in which it is accomplished. Thus, if two children paint pictures in the same amount of time, one big and one smaller, the judgement is often that the big picture took longer. Other judgements can be affected by size; a taller person may be considered older than a shorter person.

The young child will not be 'talked out' of this way of thinking. He is unable to view time objectively at this stage. Drawing the child's attention to relevant experiences, however, will help to develop his understanding; it is useful for instance to draw attention to fixed points in the day and the pattern of the week. When listening to the child's comparisons and questioning about his reasons for his decisions, the teacher can monitor progression in understanding.

Early logic

The young child develops a mastery of his world as he becomes able to predict and understand cause and effect. His logical thinking develops as he starts to distinguish differences and similarities in things and to arrange them accordingly. He also starts to see an order in these differences and begins to place items in sequences.

Initial sorting and classifying are random. When the child begins to apply logic he may sort a pile of buttons into many small groups according to size, colour and shape. Gradually, though, he is able to reduce the number of groups, and buttons may then be sorted according to one common attribute – all green buttons, whatever shape or size, together.

The ability to sequence depends on children being able to recognize differences and compare them. Through using structured fitting and grading apparatus the young child starts to order because of practicalities. For instance, a set of graded building-blocks can be built into a tower only if the largest forms the base. From experiencing this apparatus children move to ordering unstructured materials and become more and more adept at recognizing fine distinctions.

Through these experiences children learn to use some of the following words and phrases: 'belongs to', 'fits', 'does not fit', 'if', 'this will happen', 'when', 'why', 'what'. The three- to five-year-old thus develops the skills of prediction, classification and sequencing; full understanding is accomplished at a later stage. The aim of the nursery teacher should be to provide the environment and teaching to help the child make better judgements and to use these skills in solving problems.

Early number

In the past any early mathematics in the nursery tended to focus on developing number skills: 'Time is devoted to getting young children to repeat the number names, mime the number sequence, and even draw the number symbols. Unfortunately, such activities have no bearing on a child's acquisition of mathematics or appreciation of the "numberness of number".'[33] However, if seen as just one of the broad headings for developing early mathematical thinking, there is a place for young children to be introduced to numbers. The essential sub-skills to be learnt are one-to-one correspondence and conservation. At the same time, by the attachment of number names to objects and experiences some early understanding of cardinal and ordinal numbers can develop.

Given many different opportunities to match one item against another, the young child gradually comes to understand that although the objects are different in type they can be the same in number. By pairing one chair to each child, one knife to each plate and one lid for each pan the nursery teacher gives the child a concrete experience for checking that they are 'the same'; there are more chairs or less plates. Piaget contended that the young child is unable to 'conserve' – that is, to appreciate that a number of objects or an amount remains the same regardless of how it is arranged or divided up. Again, current thinking suggests that children are able to be more open-minded about this in particular circumstances (see page 62), but the nursery must concentrate on helping children to experience conservation in a range of different situations. The most effective experiences are for children to handle materials for themselves, matching and comparing quantities. As their understanding develops, they learn to match items in pictures and to see for themselves that six sausages remain the same whether arranged in a line or a circle. Young children enjoy learning number names in rhymes and activities. However, ability to count does not necessarily mean that the child can attach a meaningful number label to a concrete group of items. Counting should be incorporated into the nursery session, with the teacher encouraging the child to count an object only once. As the child starts to place items in sequence, ordinal number labels can be attached. Again, understanding develops soundly only if the child makes his own order and attaches his own labels. The teacher is wise to accept this order and naming from the child even if it is incorrect. She may, however, gently offer her own model of counting or suggest that another child finds out if he comes to the same conclusions. While all these early number skills are in an embryonic stage it is important to go along with the child, observing his mode of thinking and providing appropriate new experiences at opportune moments to help clarify or challenge his conclusions.

Although we agree that drilling young children in number does not enhance their understanding of numeracy, recent studies have challenged Piaget's views on children's arithmetical abilities. Martin Hughes's work has revealed that nursery-age children are capable of representing number symbols, albeit in an idiosyncratic way but recognizable to themselves after a week. He also found that children were capable of understanding the use of the symbols + and − under certain conditions, although they could not generalize that understanding.[34] These findings point to the need for nursery teachers to explore their children's levels of understanding in a more open-minded way.

The nursery can thus provide a seedbed for mathematical thinking. A range of potentially helpful activity can be explored, but as with other aspects of development the cue must come mainly from the child. These cues need to be observed, then taken up and developed by the teacher.

Suggested action

Provide activities with potential for mathematical development

- Spatial awareness:
  - paper and construction materials of different shapes and sizes for painting, drawing and model-making;
  - different shaped cutters for use with clay and dough;
  - small-scale play figures (dolls' house, farm and road layouts) to be arranged and rearranged in different ways.
- The beginnings of measurement: provision of apparatus and materials of different sizes to invite comparisons; e.g. two planks of unequal length for large construction; long and short brushes for painting; small and large mats for music and movement.
- The beginnings of logic: encourage pattern-making which invites children to think 'what comes next?'; e.g. teacher starts a two-colour bead pattern – child continues it; child makes his own mosaic grid pattern and asks his friend to copy it; child makes his own collection of stones while on a walk and arranges his pattern, which is then displayed with the stone patterns from the rest of the group.
- The beginnings of number:
  - sorting of miniature play figures and animals; e.g. dolls' house furniture into appropriate rooms; animals into barns and fields.
  - conservation of number in making the same number of bricks into different shapes;
  - matching socks, shoes; lotto games matching pictures, textures and symbols.

Provide stories, songs and rhymes to introduce mathematical thinking

- Spatial awareness: 'The Three Billy Goats Gruff', 'Jack and Jill Went up the Hill'.
- The beginnings of measurement: 'Goldilocks and the Three Bears', 'The Magic Porridge Pot'.
- The beginnings of logic: 'The Enormous Turnip', 'The Little Gingerbread Boy'.
- The beginnings of number: a range of rhymes involving cardinal and ordinal numbers in ascending and descending order, e.g. 'One Man Went to Mow a Meadow', 'Five Currant Buns in a Baker's Shop', 'Oats and Beans and Barley Grow'.

Provide a classroom environment and routines to encourage mathematical thinking

- Spatial awareness:
  - levels of display and storage and the creation of different learning areas should help children to look at their classroom from different spatial viewpoints;
  - setting up a 'moving day' into the home corner will encourage children to fit and rearrange furniture into a limited space;
  - sitting on the carpet for a story means that the children must ensure that there is space for everyone.
- The beginnings of measurement:
  - make a pictorial chart of the pattern of the day; regularly draw children's attention to the sequence of events until they accommodate it;
  - allow children to mix up their own glue and paint using a simple pictorial recipe; encourage them to see what happens when more or less liquid is added.
- The beginnings of logic:
  - help children to talk about cause and effect; e.g. if a vase is cracked what will happen to the water? If a beaker is filled to the brim with water what is likely to happen when it is picked up? What happens if you go out in the rain without a coat?;
  - help children to sort and classify when they put things away; e.g. by providing clearly labelled storage containers for materials

with different attributes; by clearly marking a shelf with outlines of where the containers are to be stored in order of size.

- The beginnings of number: encourage routines which involve one-to-one correspondence; e.g. children to play board – or card-games which involve them handing out one card to each person; children to hand out paintings to others at the end of the day (one to one or many to one) or to distrbute one card to each child at the end of the cookery session.

Key questions to promote mathematical thinking

- Spatial awareness: 'Where does this go?' 'How can this fit?' 'Why doesn't this fit?'
- The beginnings of measurement: 'Are they the same?' 'How can you make them the same?' 'How can you make this one smaller?'
- The beginnings of logic: 'Why do you think that has happened?' 'What will happen now?' 'Can we do that another way?'
- The beginnings of number: 'Where does that belong?' 'Is there enough for everyone?' 'What comes next?'

A BROAD CURRICULUM

We have considered the earliest ways in which young children acquire information and make sense of this information through talk and play. However, these are only some of the ways in which the child assimilates information and experience. Piaget refers to the stage of 'symbolic representations', indicating that the child is now able to understand that the symbol will stand for the experience he has had.[35] Spontaneous play is one way children symbolically represent experience through first imitating what they have seen and heard and later extending these imitations into role-play. As the child develops he is able to extend his range of symbolic representations, using the materials he has explored.

Children need access to a variety of media and activities and the opportunity to represent their understandings in the ways which make sense to them. Representation is not a matter of copying an adult, whether in dance, drawing or making a model. The teacher can nevertheless help the child refine and extend his own representations by guiding and suggesting:

- by teaching the sub-skills of handling tools, mixing and managing materials;

- by encouraging the child to talk through his activity;
- by encouraging the child to combine materials and link different ways of representing experiences;
- by responding to the child's wish to develop his representation.

The main areas of representation are the following.

Painting and drawing

The child's first attempts at writing in fact begin when he attempts visual representations. Kenneth Jameson describes communication through and about graphic expression as a beginning of academic learning.[36] The teacher should ensure that a variety of thick and fine crayons, charcoal, chalk, lead pencils and felt-tip pens are freely available, together with paper of different sizes, shapes and colours. The wider the choice of materials available, the more children will be able to select the most suitable media for their explorations and experiments.

The accent should be on individual discovery, although the teacher may need to help and encourage the less adventurous child by demonstrating the different effects that can be produced by different media. She may also want occasionally to structure the activity by limiting paint colours or drawing tools, to encourage children to explore the possibilities of using only a few.

Three-dimensional model-making

After sticking junk together randomly and setting up and knocking down piles of bricks, the child will start to use these materials for a preconceived purpose.

Construction may involve children working alone or co-operatively. Large block constructions are more likely to involve a group of children and to lead to social interaction and imaginative play. Small-scale construction will attract the solitary child, who may seek this as a quiet activity away from the group.

In exploratory construction the process is all-important, but when the child actually creates something he is likely to be more interested in the end product. Occasionally a child's intentions may prove to be somewhat ambitious practically. The child recognizes that his double-decker bus is far from complete and energy is running dry. When this happens the adult can decide whether the work is best left to be continued or if she should help the child to complete his model, making it clear to the group that 'John and I made this together'.

Making sounds

After children have had the opportunity to explore a variety of home-made and commercial percussion instruments they may use them to represent sound effects in stories or to depict some recent shared experience. For example, after children have listened to heavy rain pattering on the roof they may select shakers filled with sand or dried peas to represent the sound; or, if the sound of thunder has frightened some children, the teacher may help them play out their fears by talking through with them how they could best represent the noise, given the sounds that they make with their body or with instruments.

Young children's musical abilities develop through playing with sounds, inventing songs and using sounds to represent actions.

Dance and movement

Stories and experiences may be represented later through the child's own imitations or through teacher-initiated activities. When observing a cat the teacher may ask the children to note how the animal moves, curls up and washes itself. Movement is closely linked to all sorts of sound-making, as children use both to recall an experience. The teacher may notice the children watching the wind moving the trees outside, and by providing background music may suggest that the children imitate the actions of the branches. Large ring games, jingles and rhymes all provide opportunities for children to represent actions in different ways. The provision of simple props offers further stimulus; for example, a story about the magic shoes which made their owner into a beautiful dancer – the shoes can then be left in the home corner.

Looking at pictures and written symbols

By the time they enter the nursery, children should be able to recognize pictures and photographs as representations of real things. They may spend time looking at picture books and labelling items. At a later stage they may be able to relate photographs to their own recent experiences of an outing. Many opportunities for talk are possible, with children interpreting messages from pictures and the adult and other children listening and responding. Through these opportunities, and given experiences of stories, songs and poems, children move towards the interpretation and early representation of written symbols.[37] The teacher can use many and varied opportunities to read stories to children, at the same time following a line of print with her finger. She may write down children's descriptions of their paintings and models, showing how their talk can be represented on paper. She may make a display of children's work with their names and with their captions.

When surrounded by these symbols, the young child will start to extend his visual representations to include his own 'writing'. Marie Clay suggests several common features that children demonstrate when starting to write.[38] In the nursery some children are likely to use the symbols that they have learnt to recognize, reproducing them in different combinations and repetitions to generate a message. These early messages may lack directionality and may be quite indecipherable to the adult when they are the child's first attempts to represent letter shapes. However, the child may be able to interpret his writing, and these products can be made into the child's first books.

Suggested action

Make it possible for the child to represent

- Check the number of ways in which children are able to represent in your nursery during the course of a term.
- Make sure that there is access to a variety of materials in each area of representation; e.g. a child modelling with junk may also require fabrics, paper and drawing materials.
- Provide sufficient materials; e.g. a few large blocks or one small construction-set may be limiting for the child's intentions.

Teach the sub-skills required for making representations

- After children have explored applying paint to paper they should have the chance of mixing their own colours on a palette.
- Teach a range of simple painting techniques, e.g. printing, wax resist, for the child to choose his means of representation.
- Provide a range of brushes of different thicknesses to allow the addition of fine detail to pictures if required.
- Teach the correct handling of woodwork tools including fixing wood into a vice.
- Provide the means of quickly fixing one surface to another; e.g. pre-cut lengths of masking tape attached to a saucer may enable children to assemble things with the minimum frustration.
- Provide opportunities for children to practise copying rhythms with their body and with instruments.

- Play games which require children to imitate and create different sounds; e.g. Simon says . . . 'Growl like a dog.'
- Provide a simple playback cassette player with a range of cassettes that children are encouraged to use for themselves for dancing.
- Teach book-handling skills, e.g. how to turn pages, how to hold a book, how to return it carefully to the bookshelf.
- After reading a story, leave it in a prominent position – it is likely to be selected by a child who will 'read' it to his friends.

Encourage the child to talk through his activity

- Avoid 'what is it?' questions but instead pick out one feature of the child's painting to comment on; e.g. 'What a lovely colour blue in that part of your picture, Leon. Can you tell me about that?'
- Some children will want to outline their mental plan before starting work. Help by asking supplementary questions: 'So where will the people sit in this bus? . . . I see, and where is the engine going to be?'
- Puppet-making is an ideal way of helping a child to express his thoughts through a model. Simple puppets can be made from socks or cross-pieces of folded newspaper. You need to talk with the children through your own puppet used in activities and at story time in order to offer a model.
- Have home-made shakers which have different sound effects; each child can ask the others in a small group to close their eyes and guess what his sound represents. This is not easy and will require encouragement and sensitive contributions from you to help children listen and then relate the sound to a past experience.
- Give help initially to the child to interpret his actions into words: 'Oh Sam, you have curled up in that barrel like a little tight ball. Can you make yourself even smaller?'
- Encourage the children to see print as a means of gaining information; e.g. provide simple pictorial cookery recipes for them to read; pictorial and print instructions for mixing paint and clay.

Encourage the child to combine materials and to link his representations

If children have had a range of experiences, they will start to select the most appropriate media for a particular representation they have in mind.

- Provide activities which suggest combining materials, e.g. pieces of card, a selection of powder paint to be mixed, adhesive, lengths of wool, silver paper and pieces of cork. If there are requests for additional materials, so much the better.
- Provide books and writing materials in the home area.
- Encourage one representation to lead to another; e.g. 'Oh Sandra, that boat looks really good. Would you like to make a special harbour for it in the construction area?'

Encourage the child to develop his representation

This should be tackled with care. Be aware that the child might be quite satisfied with his product.

- Help the recall of detail; e.g. 'Your dad looks very happy in that picture, Peter. Was he wearing shoes, I wonder?'
- Provide reference material in the way of books, charts and pictures.
- Encourage completion over a period of time; e.g. older children may prefer to leave a model they are making for a few days and then return to it.
- Encourage close observations of real objects with attention to detail.
- Suggest elaborations. Once the child is creating rhythms, speed and volume can also be introduced; e.g. 'That horse sounds really good, Sally' (using coconut shells). 'Can we make him sound slow and weary now? He is a long way away, so we can only just hear him.'

A BALANCED CURRICULUM

So far we have looked at the child's mental development and how this is nurtured. A balanced curriculum, however, considers the whole child and all aspects of development.

The first point to make is perhaps that raised in *The Practical Curriculum*: 'For the children themselves the effective curriculum is what each child takes away. Schools and their teachers need ways of finding out what each child's experience is and how well they are learning what the school intends.'[39] The teacher should be aware that there may be a great discrepancy between her planning for children and the benefit the children receive. She may have provided an attractive sensory area with 'feely' bags and a range of interesting artefacts for children to touch, only to find that very few children have approached the area.

What the individual child receives depends on his individual stage of development and personal motivation. A large group activity poses a particular challenge in ensuring that twenty or thirty egocentric individuals benefit in their learning. For example, the teacher may aim to teach a song. Within her group there are likely to be children who are ready to receive group instruction; they are capable of both learning the words and enjoying the joint singing. At the other extreme are those with a very limited concentration span who find it difficult to sit still for more than a few minutes; they may not be ready to cope with language from an adult other than on a one-to-one basis. These children may learn other things than what is intended. They may learn from one another by chatting together; they may become skilful at avoiding the teacher's attention by positioning themselves on the outer fringe of the group, requesting to go to the lavatory or keeping quiet while effectively shutting themselves off from an activity that is meaningless for them.

Once again we turn to individual need, because the appropriate curriculum will differ for each child. A balanced provision allows for individual choice, individual need and different levels of learning. Balance also allows for children to play by themselves or in pairs and to be introduced to being one of a group. It ensures an environment that challenges the most confident and reassures the besitant child who is hovering on the threshold of learning.

Perhaps a pertinent question is what should be left out of this curriculum. Are we in danger of encompassing everything and ending up with a piecemeal and overcrowded curriculum? Children of this age benefit from exposure to a wealth of experiences and being given the means to represent the experiences in as many ways as possible, thus exercising their mental, physical and creative skills. This approach develops a sound platform for further learning.

However, if coherent and all-round development is to be achieved, the programme should consider home experiences. The extent to which a child may be allowed to play outside on large apparatus day after day can vary. If that child lives in a small flat with no outside play space, or if he is urged to spend his time at home on passive, sedentary activities, this will affect the nursery teacher's decision. But the need to know about home life-style is important only as it is seen to affect the child's learning. Equally important is the teacher's careful continual assessment of developmental strengths and weaknesses on which to base a balanced learning programme. While there should be ample opportunity for the child to enjoy and practise what he is good at, the teacher should intervene sensitively to rectify weakness. This skill requires that the teacher select curriculum content and method that particularly motivates that child. If for instance a child's manipulative skills are weak, and he chooses to spend most of his time playing in the home area, the teacher should see that dolls and teddies are dressed in clothes with buttons, zips and fasteners and that one doll has long hair which invites plaiting.

A balanced curriculum requires both short-term and long-term planning. What are the extended experiences and consequent learning for the child over a period of a week, a term and a year? There should be opportunities for both child-initiated and adult-directed activity, the balance being determined by recognition of the gains offered to children by each approach.

A balanced programme allows for both sedentary and active physical play, for large group activity as well as quiet areas to allow the solitary child to withdraw from noise and activity. The primacy of first-hand experience has been stressed, but there is also a real place for second-hand experiences, from listening to stories and music. Varied provision needs to be balanced with fixed curricular points. Children will respond to new stimulus, but some need to know that the painting area or the home bay is constant. The adequacy of any structured learning programme must be considered in the light of the aim to provide for the whole child. The United States High Scope programme, whilst providing a good framework for children's cognitive development, does not acknowledge the place for the child's emotional growth or the time needed to adapt to a new nursery environment. Montessori methods provide for well-structured and sequenced activities but leave no room for individual spontaneity. A balanced curriculum should take the best of all approaches and use them, when appropriate, for each child.

If a balanced curriculum is considered over a period, there is no need for concern about having all tools of learning available for children all the time. There are obvious benefits in allowing children to sustain an interest even if this means that other forms of activity are temporarily ignored. There is occasionally a place for strictly limiting material for play. One nursery contacted other establishments in its area and arranged to borrow all available bricks and blocks. Having gathered a wide range, the nursery environment was set out using just these materials; small bricks were placed on tables and mats, and, using all available space inside and outside, large blocks were attractively displayed. The children had been forewarned of a 'different day' but nevertheless some took time to adjust to the new environment. However, at the end of the session, the staff were clear about the benefits. Children who had never been seen to play with blocks before co-operated together to plan and build; the quality of some language and intricacy of some of the constructions was impressive, and most of the children were very enthusiastic about the day. Freed from the managerial demands of overseeing a range of activities, the adults were able to observe individual children closely and had time to be involved with their play. Thus another dimension of the balanced curriculum is the creation of contrasting atmospheres and environments, from which both children and adults may benefit.

Suggested action

Ensure that the children are affected by the teacher's intentions

- When you have read or told a story, observe how many children in the group refer to that story at a later date, or show any signs of representing the characters or play through other activities. Repeat the story-telling with very small groups of children/at a different time of day/using different content. Check the effects on the children again.
- How many children use the art area during the day? If it is underused, try:
  - changing its position in the nursery;
  - briefing a group of children about some new colour paint that you have set out and showing them the effects they can create using different sized brushes;
  - suggesting that the children themselves set up a new art area, deciding where it will be and what will be laid out.
- Ask parents what their children talk about at home relating to nursery activities (see Chapter 3 for further discussion of parent involvement).

Provide for different groupings during the session

- Check how many activities encourage children to work in pairs; e.g. cookery – making edible people or animals from icing sugar and whisked egg white, chairs and aprons laid out for two; table game with two sets of counters.
- Check the provision for a child who wishes to retreat; e.g. a large sturdy three-sided carton furnished with cushions and a curtain draped over for privacy.

Ensure that the curriculum is rectifying weaknesses

- Identify the children who rarely play with water and see that they have similar exploratory experiences using dry sand.
- Check that these children's hand/eye co-ordination skills are developed by pouring tea in the home corner or milk at break time.
- Introduce these children to water by asking them to wash up the paint pots or wipe down the tables after activities.

Vary the teaching rhythm

- Simplify the regime to allow children occasionally to explore and represent in one medium.
- Have one session a term when you focus on one activity; e.g. imitative and role-play – small-scale fantasy play using miniature layouts, people and animals.

INDEPENDENCE AND AUTONOMY

Young children need to become agents in their own learning. A young child's level of dependence is greatly affected by his inherited endowment as well as by the style of parenting. Studies have indicated the effects of restricting toddlers from normal developmental experiences such as climbing stairs and exploring objects, or of other extreme behaviour in pushing two- and three-year-olds towards more mature habits; both these attitudes are likely to cause overdependency.[40] The development of independence is aided by a degree of permissiveness and warmth rather than punitive treatment.[41] Erikson writes that the first task of facing a child's personality is to learn to trust.[42] When he is assured that his physical and emotional needs are being met by an adult, he is then able to turn his attention to the wider world.

On entry to nursery school children vary in their adaptation and activity. Each child has his own stage of readiness with regard to developing emotional independence from his parents, being socially confident in mixing and co-operating with peers, and being physically capable and intellectually self-reliant in making choices, solving problems and initiating actions. All these aspects of autonomous development are important, but Lesley Webb argues particularly for intellectual autonomy:

> It is precisely in encouraging rational, personal autonomy (i.e. the ability of a young child to think for himself) that the nursery school or class has its most

> important function . . . It certainly requires of an adult more skill and knowledge to help a child to think something out for himself than to help him to be independent in washing or dressing, yet the two roles of the adult as the two different kinds of self-reliance are easily confused.[43]

Lesley Webb argues that intellectual autonomy can be fostered only by the teacher, whereas a nursery assistant or untrained helper is more capable of fostering social and physical independence. This polarization is perhaps questionable, because these aspects of development are interwoven. The nursery teacher must expect to spend more of her time with the child who is emotionally over-dependent. The researchers concerned with the transition study found it somewhat surprising that the total adult time given to all new children was less than 10 per cent.[44] Some new children and less confident 'established' children undoubtedly benefit from a more obvious staff presence in helping them to understand the nursery setting and to take an active part in it. The parent substitute should thus be available to each individual as long as she is needed. Social dependence is closely related to emotional stability. An anxious, insecure child will have difficulty in relating to new adults or children. However, a child who is highly dependent on the nursery adult may not find it so easy to relate to other children.

The skills of making and maintaining friendships in the nursery are many and complex. They include the ability to offer friendship, manage conflicts and maintain one's rights while being sensitive to those others.[45] Although the child will learn many skills from his peers, the adult should engineer situations to help children who are in danger of becoming isolates. Any special circumstances need to be considered. As we have seen, a new child may need initially to spend a considerable amount of time 'on the fringe' of activities, watching the play of other children before he can take part. Social interaction also depends on the stage of development and the personality of the child. A child of two years will normally play by himself and be unable to co-operate with others, but solitary play in four-year-olds is related to dependency; if this is a persistent and dominant form of play it is likely to relate to a poor self-image and to a low level of attention-seeking. However, where a four-year-old plays alone and actively resists any interference this can reflect purposeful play and a level of sociability.

Carefully monitored group activity enables children to grow from an egocentric state to become group members. In their play children learn to lead, to follow and co-operate, to wait and take turns. Opportunities for this type of growth need to be an integral part of a nursery programme. Where children find this learning particularly difficult, specific planning should provide for individual need. In helping children develop social skills the teacher must be aware that not all people are capable of being, or even wish to be, friendly and outgoing. However, the nursery has responsibility to provide children with a range of life skills. If a child is able to communicate and interact easily with others he may still choose his own company, but the child who lacks these social skills does not have this choice.

A degree of physical independence assists all young children in gaining confidence. The three-year-old who can cope with his own personal needs ceases to look to the teacher to support him in this aspect of his life. For this reason games need to be played which teach the fastening of buttons and buckles; painting aprons need to have strips of Velcro which the child can fix for himself; the teacher should ensure that small fingers can attach paper to painting easels by means of clothes pegs and that there is an accessible line where the child can place his painting to dry after completing it. Routines should also encourage physical self-control; given conveniently located cloakrooms, nursery children can be encouraged to visit the lavatory as and when needed rather than automatically responding to group set times during the day.

Nurseries need to provide a climate in which a young child can develop emotional resilience and become socially and physically confident before he can develop his thinking skills. Helping young children to take responsibility for their actions involves them in making choices and decisions. They need to be helped to take an increasingly active part in their own learning, and the teacher's planning and provision can assist this process in the following ways.

Choosing play materials

There needs to be an opportunity for children to select their resources for learning. Open, low shelves with apparatus in pictorially coded containers with well-fitted lids mean that play materials are accessible. As children become familiar with using different media for creative work they develop discrimination and are able to choose and reject materials as being more or less appropriate for their particular work. A range of paper of different shapes, sizes, textures and colours should be adjacent to the painting area; a choice of adhesives and a selection of materials for collage should also be freely available. This type of provision will help to enhance the learning opportunities in these activities.

Allocation of time

The nursery session should be planned to enable the child to have choice in his use of time. If a midmorning snack is provided on a self-service basis, the arrangement allows a child to break off an activity when he is ready, pour his drink for himself and decide what quantity he can manage. Many children initially need help in planning their time; a rich provision of activities can be indigestible for an individual who has had no experience of making decisions at home.

Choice of activities

There may be opportunities for children to choose whether to play indoors or outside and whether to take part in a large group story or music session or to opt for a more solitary occupation. Even the youngest children can be helped to make decisions about their environment and daily activities. A new sand tray arrives; suggestions may be made as to where it can best be sited. The cookery activity for tomorrow can be decided by the group browsing over a pictorial recipe book. Which paintings and models to display in the nursery can be a group decision, as can the selection of seeds to be planted in the garden and the choice of material for new curtains in the home area.

Apart from her provision the teacher's own attitudes are all-important. With the high demands of teaching this age group it is tempting to reward conforming and complacent behaviour in children. However, in returning to main principles, if the accent is to be on developing personal, rational autonomy the teacher must positively encourage independent thinkers, those who question authoritative statements and sometimes choose to tackle things differently.

The US High Scope programme helps children to accept responsibility for their actions. They are encouraged to make choices about their activities, to carry out these plans and then to discuss the outcomes with an adult.[46] This approach appears to have value in placing the child in an active learning position. However, no one system should become a strait-jacket; there is a great difference between seeing the High Scope method as a useful way of helping children to become agents in their learning and imposing this framework on all children. As we have seen, emotional and social confidence is necessary before any child is ready to make choices and decisions about learning. Whatever the activity structure, it should not be allowed to inhibit spontaneity and creativity, which are often the keys to development.

Suggested action

Help the child to trust

- Aim to be in the same place every day at the start of every session to welcome the children.
- Be aware when one child feels particularly vulnerable, e.g. transition, large group time or an outing; use eye contact and physical touch to assure the child of your support.
- Find a special puppet for the insecure child. Make sure that the puppet is 'put to bed' by the child when he leaves the nursery and is waiting for that child the next morning when he arrives.
- Try to introduce the child to another adult at an early stage. A mother substitute is all-important at first, but the aim must be for trust to be established within the wider circle.

Help the child become socially adept

- Introduce two isolated children to a task in the hope that they will support one another.
- Help children to learn social skills; e.g. ensure that attention-seeking children have initial brief experiences when they must wait for the adult – praise warmly as the attention-seeking becomes less; encourage and help children to take turns.
- Offer children leadership roles; e.g. 'Now Tony, you tell us where we are going in this aeroplane.'
- Encourage children to support one another; e.g. suggest that a child bathes a friend's sore knee or helps another clear up a breakage.

Develop self-help skills

- Resource the environment to allow children to become self-sufficient; e.g. provide a dustpan and brush for clearing up dry sand; provide a floor cloth or short-handled mop for coping with spillages.
- Have clear expectations for children and support them in achieving these; e.g. encourage children to take responsibility for their own possessions (clipping wellington boots together with a named

wooden peg); give children areas of responsibility such as keeping the book area tidy or checking the painting aprons for repairs; one activity should be tidied away before moving on to another.
- Communicate to parents in the hope that these expectations will be supported at home.

LEARNING SUCCEEDS THROUGH SUCCESS

Nursery teachers accept that young children make mistakes and learn valuable lessons in this way. Children must also learn that in many matters there are no right or wrong answers. However, to foster children who are confident to 'have a go' and express their views and eager to explore new learning, a nursery curriculum must allow children to experience success, and these successful experiences should outweigh all others. The learning offered must therefore be manageable and broken into manageable segments. The great skill of teaching at any level is to facilitate learning: to identify what has been previously learnt and the next required step in learning; to find the right match of curriculum content and the appropriate learning route. It is impossible to provide a correct match for all children all the time, but reflections on why an approach did not work with a child, or why a line of enquiry proved especially successful, are the very essence of self-evaluation (see Chapter 5).

The particular skill of the nursery teacher lies in getting to know about the competencies of her age group of children. In judging what a young child understands, the teacher needs to know about his past experiences and observe his use of oral language and his actions. In this work it is important to consider recent research findings, which emphasize the need to place nursery children in the best possible position for them to demonstrate their understanding. Some of these findings question the work of Piaget and his consequent conclusions about children's competencies. While Piaget stressed the kind of thinking that young children could not manage, current studies indicate that, given the appropriate working conditions, these same children are capable of functioning at a much higher level.

One major finding of Piaget's was that most children younger than seven are unable to appreciate another point of view – they are totally egocentric.[47] The test for this was to show the young child a three-dimensional model of a mountain with three distinctly different sides, to place the child on one side of the mountain and put a small doll looking at a different side.

The child was then given three photographs showing each perspective of the mountain and was asked to select the view that the doll had. On this standard test most children under seven are unable to select the correct photograph; most selected the view that they had. Borke repeated this test, but instead of the photographs the child was asked to demonstrate the doll's view by turning the mountain, which was mounted on a turntable. Using this means many four-year-olds and some children of three were able to select the correct side of the mountain.[48] Thus, given the opportunity to express their understanding appropriately, young children will, it seems, give us a clearer picture of their capabilities. Their thinking will be better expressed if they are dealing with a familiar situation. Borke continued to modify Piaget's test by using the turntable but substituting animals and people in home settings in place of the mountain. This situation was presumably more like home than the Swiss Alps, and even more children responded favourably to seeing another viewpoint.

A further point regarding young children's thinking relates to their understanding of our intentions. In Piaget's experiment on conservation, children were asked to check two sets of five counters. When the sets were aligned, the children said that they were the same; when the second set of counters was pushed apart by the teacher, the children mainly considered that this second row contained more counters.[49] In a modified version of this test McGarrigle used a naughty teddy to push the counters apart and shuffle them around. This time more children gave the correct response than in the previous test.[50]

Margaret Donaldson contends that young children's actions are affected by them trying to make sense of human situations and of people's intentions.[51] She suggests that in the Piagetian test the child tries to make sense of the adult's intention by drawing on his experience of them usually doing something for a purpose. Thus, the child's expectation would be that the adult had caused something to happen. With the introduction of a naughty teddy the children were more likely to be open-minded about the result of his actions.

Young children's understanding of the teacher's use of language is also important – the way the adult phrases her talk. Margaret Donaldson suggests that a young child may be seen to fail to carry out a task or to respond to an instruction, not because he is incapable of that task but because he cannot comprehend the adult's use of language.

Children are better placed to reveal their competencies if they are given the means to express their understanding, if they are dealing with a situation that is familiar to them and if they can make sense of the adult's use of language. If the teacher is to move close to the child's thinking she should be aware that young children comprehend their surroundings by making their own meanings which are consistent in their own terms. These meanings are not always clear to adults. The teacher needs to get inside the child's own frame of reference. Vygotsky's statement made more than fifty years ago is still relevant: 'It is not sufficient to understand his words – we must also understand his thoughts. But even that is not enough – we must also know its motivation. No analysis of an utterance is complete until that plane is reached.'[52]

One of the most effective ways of getting close to a child's thinking is through dialogue. David Woods suggests that 'Conversations with young children at best give an insight into their needs, feelings, fears and attitudes. They are a primary basis for reaching an understanding of each child.'[53] But, as Woods points out, not all adults have the natural ability to handle the demands of conversation with a group of young children effectively. It is a skill for the nursery teacher to refine and use as a major tool of work. It is one thing to get a child to talk but quite another to involve and interest him in a sustained conversation. Most young children, given a gently persistent questioner, will respond, but the response is likely to be limited to answering the question.

Woods describes the 'programmatic' style of conversation, which consists of the adult asking questions and the child replying. Thus the dialogue at a dough table may be:

Teacher: 'What are you making, Rachel?'
Child: 'Eggs.'
Teacher: 'Oh, they do look nice. How many are you making?'
(No response.)
Teacher: 'How many, Rachel?'
Child: 'Two.'
Teacher: 'Yes, and what colour are they?'
Child: 'Red.'

The teacher is evidently working hard, but to little effect. The child feels under pressure to answer and is feeding back the minimum information. The teacher controls the conversation, and the child plays a secondary, responsive role. Woods's analysis of many transcripts of conversations shows that where the adult or teacher had less of a controlling style of conversation, children asked more questions and made more contributions of their own. From this study he suggests that adults who offer children their own views and ideas receive a great deal more from children.

Thus we may see a rather different approach to conversation at the dough table.

Teacher: 'Oh, those look interesting, Rachel. They are like some red marbles that I played with when I was a little girl.'
Child: 'Was you a little girl?'
Teacher: 'Yes, just like you, with long hair.'
Child: 'When you was a little girl, does you . . . does you play?'
Teacher: 'Oh yes, I played with lots of things. But I didn't play with dough.'
Child: 'I made one dough with Jason. Jason made it blue . . . Jason made it all blue . . . His hands was blue . . . My mum . . . mum was cross 'cos it was all blue and Jason cried.'
Teacher: 'Oh dear, paint can be very messy. I expect it was a bit difficult for your mum to clear it up.'

The adult's use of language will change according to circumstances. There is a place for questioning a child and for giving direct instructions. The very pace of work often dictates the need for a brief response to a child. However, here we are considering how it is possible to place children in the best possible circumstances to enable them to voice their views and feelings, and this is most likely to be achieved by the teacher adopting a partnership approach in conversation.

A great deal of work has focused on early language development through adult–child interaction, but less attention has been paid to children talking together. Yet nursery settings put a great deal of emphasis on making this possible through the arrangement of furniture and the organization of activities. Although one of the aims of nursery provision is to help the child become socially confident, as Sylva suggests, 'A child's social participation is not only the "classroom" for acquiring interpersonal skills, it is also the scene of his most complex and creative thought.'[54]

Robson's study of nursery children talking together involved recording dialogue by means of attaching radio microphones to target children. The work suggests that younger, more immature children learn a great deal from older peers both by imitating their actions and language and also through being directly taught by older children. Children are often also very good at understanding another child's indistinct speech which an adult may find incomprehensible.

Robson suggests that teachers can learn a great deal by studying children's conversations. Ideally this means recording the dialogue and studying transcripts afterwards. However, recognizing the difficulties in managing this, Robson believes that certain points arising from her own study are applicable to other nursery settings. One major factor was the complexity of children's language used in conversation with one another. Robson suggests that teachers tend to use simple, concrete language, being aware of their least capable children in the nursery. Inevitably the children with good linguistic skills are not stretched; these children often appeared to avoid or misunderstand adult conversations, probably, the author suggests, because they were bored with the lack of challenge.

A further point reinforces Woods's work on dialogue. Children's conversations with one another contrasted starkly with adult–child talk. Children's conversations wee more on the lines of balanced conversation, but adult–child talk tended to focus on questions and answers.

Robson says that by observing children's talk it is possible to deduce the best settings to promote the richest exchanges.[55] Sylva's study found that in the Oxford nursery classes there was a particularly high incidence of children conversing with one another. Sylva concludes that one reason for this was the popular provision for manipulative activities and pretend play, which provide excellent settings for dialogue.

Perhaps the key ingredient in enabling children to succeed is the role motivation plays in learning. This must surely be a priority for any nursery teacher and a particular challenge in view of the very wide developmental span that she may be coping with at any one time. We have mentioned the importance of matching activities and methods to each child's need. Children can respond to very challenging learning if the approach is interesting and enticing. Martin Hughes successfully introduced a group of four-year-olds to the code of arithmetic. He found that they were capable of understanding and using a simple form of arithmetical symbolism and he attributed this success to the work being introduced through an enjoyable game. Hughes reports that by his final session the children were as keen to participate in the game as they were in the beginning, if not keener. He comments that 'Many pre-school children appear to appreciate and enjoy intellectual problems which are pitched at the limits of their understanding.'[56]

To summarize: if young children have successful experiences at the earliest stage of their education this has implications for a spiral of success at later stages in their development. Success breeds confidence and a willingness to be open to learning. To help children to be successful the nursery teacher should make their learning manageable, by breaking it down to meet individual needs, and should place children in the best possible position to reveal their learning and to express their thoughts, views and actions through talk with adults and other children. Aspects of research suggest that teachers can expect more of young children in terms of their learning as long as the teaching is embodied in exciting and relevant modes which are within the child's frame of reference.

Suggested action

Help the child express his understanding

- Observe how a child chooses to represent an experience and draw his attention back to the experience to crystallize the link; e.g. 'You are flying an aeroplane like the man in the story, Darren. Can you land in the field as he did?'
- Ask a child to show you how a model works if he is hesitant in telling how. You can then help him translate the action into language.

Plan the learning in a familiar context

When checking a child's competencies always aim to use familiar materials and to make the context of work the usual nursery setting, preferably with other children.

Help the child understand the adult's intentions

- Check that your own behaviour and comments are as consistent as possible.
- If you plan to be absent, tell the children in advance and try to explain why you will be away.

Check that the child understands the adult's use of language

- Having given an instruction, check from the child's actions that he has understood.
- On entry to the nursery, check with parents about the child's understanding of terms for going to the lavatory.
- Listen to parents talking with their children; note the use of special phrases and words.

Enable children to help one another

- Encourage one child to show another what he is doing.
- Having shown a small group of children how to use a new piece of apparatus, introduce a younger or less able child and ask the group to show him.
- Ask an able child to do specific things for a new or less able child; e.g. 'Chloe, will you do up Peter's coat, please, and show him

where to put his shoes. Alex, could you read a story to Jude and show him the pictures?'

- Refer one child to another; e.g. 'Joe is wondering where he can put this dinosaur. Sean, can you help him?'

Nurture motivation

- Keep in touch with children's interests at home.
- Observe where children choose to spend their time and follow this up; e.g. the children who build a lot can be shown some architects' plans and offered the materials to make their own.
- Observe when behaviour indicates boredom or frustration – it is the moment for adult intervention.
- Be ready to help a child through an activity; e.g. completing a jigsaw, supporting an unstable model.
- Make tasks manageable; e.g. a child may enjoy sharpening a few pencils but may want to hand over the task after a time.
- Praise generously but with discretion – children know when they have achieved.

YOUNG CHILDREN ARE PEOPLE

It has been stressed that we educate not only an intellect but the child as a whole person. Physical and psychological needs must be met if the teacher is to have children who are comfortable in body and personality.

Physical development

A child's physical growth and the way he uses his body have a very real effect on the way he operates in his environment. A child whose body hurts or bothers him or whose muscles do not function efficiently is likely to be vulnerable emotionally and is unlikely to be receptive to new learning experiences. The child's developing perceptions depend on his physical interaction with the world around him; if he is limited physically, his perceptions will be, too. For instance, the child with spina bifida who cannot lift objects will have difficulty in acquiring a concept of weight. An environment which denies children the opportunities to practise basic body skills can mean that these skills will be limited or never develop in later life. A child's progress in reading and writing can be hampered by the failure to develop certain co-ordination skills during the early years.

The child's physical build and stature can also affect functioning. Brierley, while offering no conclusive evidence about malnutrition affecting brain development, does see it as a contributory factor which can inhibit growth:

> It is hard to single out malnutrition as a cause of lowered IQ from the context of family life as a whole. Poor food is often associated with lack of play and talk and seems to be part of an impoverished syndrome, and its combined effects on mental development can be as grave as physical battering.[57]

Although the prenatal period and the first three years of life see the most rapid period of growth, between two and five years a child normally grows six inches in height and will increase approximately thirteen pounds in weight. Regular, steady gains in height are an indicator of the child's good state of health. The physical process of development from the helpless uncoordinated new-born baby to the agile, energetic and independent five-year-old is a compressed and orderly one. Normally one stage will be completed successfully before another can begin, and as with all aspects of development the rate of progress will vary according to the opportunities that the child has to acquire these skills. Mary Sheridan's guide on young children's developmental progress outlines the growth of competence in gross and fine motor skills.[58] The range of a child's gross motor movements follows on from his learning to walk. At three the child can stand and walk on tiptoe; the five-year-old can hop two or three yards forward on each foot separately. Between three and five years the child learns to skip, balance and dance to music. With fine movements the three-year-old enjoys painting with a large brush, but representational pictures do not usually occur until about four years of age. Around five years the child's hand control should be good enough for him to start to form letters (clearly this depends on whether he has had sufficient practice in the use of crayons, pencils and brushes).

The teacher needs to be aware of the stages of physical development, because part of her job should be to keep an eye on the child's health and growth. However, she must also know how to offer the best curriculum which will promote physical competence. Such provision cannot accelerate the rate of competence before the child is physiologically and psychologically ready, but the quality of movement can be refined once that stage is reached.

Gallahue sees a relationship between the quality of a child's movement and his intellectual development. He suggests that self-confidence, self-concept and readiness to explore can all be linked to the opportunities for movement and fine motor control provided at home and at school.[59] Most recent research on children's preferences for gross motor play reports that boys are predominantly interested in physical activity, as opposed to girls.[60] Wetton further concluded that the group of four-year-old boys she observed did not require large apparatus for their physical activity, but that a large space was more important. Wetton also found that three-year-olds used large apparatus more than older nursery children; she suggests that this might be because teachers were relying on the apparatus standing alone as a stimulus for the development of skills and by so doing were ignoring the significance of their own role.

The nursery teacher has a responsibility to provide for the child's physical development. It is not appropriate to have an organized lesson for gross motor development at this age, because responding to precise verbal instructions and working as a group will be beyond most children. Instead the opportunities present themselves through the environment, with the adult at hand to help refine the skill and to help the child describe what he is doing. This approach calls for an observant eye and sensitivity to intervene at the appropriate moment. Many activities for gross motor development take place out of doors, although it is important to have large physical equipment available indoors during bad weather. A child's fine motor movements develop through his developing social skills of dressing and feeding himself as well as using purpose-built apparatus and engaging in creative and messy play.

Personal and moral development

The final section of this chapter deals with the personal and moral development of young children. It has been left until last because these aspects of development must underpin all others. Surely it is the individual with the successful personality who is going to live life in its fullest sense however much we emphasize the importance of other aspects of development.

Erikson believed that each stage of childhood sets a permanent stamp on future personality. When his childhood experiences are successful a person will reach adulthood with the capacity to develop successful relationships and with the potential for working and achieving a happy, balanced existence. Where the reverse occurs, in extreme circumstances there can be an arrest of personality and the development of a pattern of behaviour which may prevent a person ever achieving his potential.[61]

The development of self-esteem is considered basic for a sound personality. The nursery teacher's job must be constantly to develop in every child a sense of being worth while. Many of the ways she tackles this have already been considered: by ensuring that he is secure and settled in his environment; by allowing him to exercise his increasing powers of independence; and by making it possible for him to succeed. The particular needs of individual children must also be taken into account. These needs may be made manifest in behaviour problems. Children may draw attention to themselves by soiling, through aggressive behaviour or pilfering. However, the teacher should not jump to conclusions about the cause of this behaviour. The arrival of a new baby in the family may be the reason for a child suddenly developing attention-seeking behaviour; on the other hand, the behaviour could be due to some totally different circumstance. The nursery teacher has a particularly difficult task here. Many attention-seeking strategies and cries for help may have adverse effects on other children. While there is a need to protect others from aggressive behaviour, the aggressive child's problem needs to be unravelled, which in some cases may require expert help from an outside agency.

The nursery child's moral judgements are in embryo. Piaget tested young children's understanding of punishment and justice by offering them pairs of stories and listening to their responses.[62] One pair of stories involved a child breaking china; in the first incident a tray of china was broken accidentally by a child who was trying to be helpful, and in the other story a cup was broken as a result of the child taking something he had been forbidden to touch. Young children believed that the child in the first story deserved the greater punishment. Their judgement was based on the seriousness of the outcome as opposed to the intentions behind the incident.

Piaget and other psychologists concerned with moral development stress the need for young children to have contact with their peers to develop moral judgements. As children socialize with one another they learn to modify their views and to consider other people's views. Moral behaviour is gradually seen as being something for the good of the group.

The child's personality and development of attitudes are also affected by the hidden curriculum in school – all the messages received by the child during the nursery day. Chapter 4 deals with the teacher's own role, but it is sufficient to say here that she must provide the model on which her children will learn to base their understanding of the world. The way young children are received into school, the way their paintings, models and conversations are received and dealt with, and the relationships teachers have with their children and parents will all affect the child as a person. The ethos of the school and its effects on the child will be tempered by the home environment. All the principles discussed can be translated into more effective practice with children if teachers can work in partnership with parents. This will be discussed in Chapter 3.

Suggested action

Plan for physical development in gross motor skills

- Check outdoor provision to see (1) the range of equipment provided to develop different body skills; (2) opportunities offered by the layout, e.g. corners for turning, marked lines for jumping, zebra crossing for stopping.
- Check indoor provision to see (1) that it is always available, e.g. opportunities to move furniture around, large play area, music-and-movement session in large group; (2) that specific opportunities are offered, e.g. obstacle course, climbing frame that can be constructed indoors as well as outdoors.
- Check that children are challenged; e.g. a visit to a park gives them the chance to run to the limit of their ability; large construction apparatus enables life-size models to be built.
- Plan for an adult role; e.g. one adult to check systematically the range of physical skills practised by a group of children in one day.

Plan for physical development in fine motor skills

- Check the skills practised during daily routines, e.g. dressing and undressing, pouring drinks, mixing paints, tidying small apparatus away.
- Plan regular practice of rhymes and jingles that involve fine motor skills.
- Check that apparatus is suitable for skill development; e.g. short painting brushes are easier to manage; fine brushes may be required by children who want to add fine detail to their pictures; inset jigsaw puzzles with knobs are easier for less mature children to handle.
- Check progression; e.g. first attempts at painting involve whole arm movements on large sheets of paper; further experiences should include experiments with a range of painting and drawing tools, being taught the correct grasp of brush/crayon, working on vertical and horizontal surfaces, tracing and drawing around objects.

Nurture self-esteem

- Ensure that a child with a poor self-image has a daily experience of succeeding that is recognized and praised.

- Give children the chance to show their achievements to others; e.g. 'Moira, Alex would like to see your model of a plane. He is making one as well.'
- Be sensitive to the child's particular need for recognition, e.g. the poorly dressed child who arrives at the nursery with a new pair of trousers.
- Always ensure that a child has a chance to right a wrong; e.g. the child who damages another's model is helped by the teacher to stick it together again.

Assist moral development

- Use real nursery experiences to pose moral problems to children; e.g. 'Dan spilt the paint. Was that naughty or just an accident?'
- Observe children's reactions and comments to note their level of thinking; e.g. Q. 'Joe pushed Peter – why?' A. 'Because Peter had taken his car.' Q. 'What else might Joe have done which would have meant not hurting Peter?'
- Note moral judgements offered by children during role-play and, where desirable, offer an opinion.

Offer positive messages through the hidden curriculum

- Give time to individual children; e.g. where possible stagger beginnings and ends of sessions to allow time for a personal greeting and farewell.
- Give children respect, e.g. by offering them undivided attention when they are talking, displaying their work with care, remembering information and views that they have previously offered.
- Make the curriculum meaningful and realistic; e.g. give children reasons for routines and rules.
- Involve children in their nursery; e.g. simple printing on lining paper can be used as new wallpaper for the home corner; a picnic outside can involve children making sandwiches to eat, having previously chosen and shopped for the ingredients. Give the children a range of choices for a simple outing; allow them to make the decisions, where practicable.

REFERENCES

1 S. Isaacs, *Intellectual Growth in Young Children*, Routledge & Kegan Paul, London, 1930.
2 S. Isaacs, *Social Development in Young Children: A Study of Beginnings*, Routledge & Kegan Paul, London, 1933.
3 B. Tizard, *Early Childhood Education*, National Foundation for Educational Research (NFER), Slough, 1974.
4 J. Brierley, *A Human Birthright: Giving the Young Brain a Chance*, British Association for Early Childhood Education, London, 1984.
5 P. Blatchford, S. Battle and J. Mays, *The First Transition: Home to Pre-School*, NFER/Nelson, Slough, 1982.
6 M. Willes, 'Children becoming pupils', in C. Alderman (ed.), *Uttering, Muttering*, Grant McIntyre, London, 1981.
7 Blatchford, Battle and Mays, op. cit. (note 5).
8 S. Cleave, S. Jowett and M. Bate, *And So to School*, NFER/Nelson, Slough, 1982.
9 J. Piaget and B. Inhelder, *The Psychology of the Child*, Basic Books, New York, 1969.
10 Brierley, op. cit. (note 4).
11 D. Ausabel *et al., Educational Psychology: A Cognitive View*, 2nd edn, Holt, Rinehart & Winston, New York, 1978.
12 C. Hutt, 'Exploration and play in children', in R.E. Herron and B. Sutton-Smith (eds.), *Child's Play*, Wiley, Chichester, 1971.
13 L.S. Vygotsky, 'Play and its role in the mental development of the child', *Voprosy Psikhologii*, 1966; from a record of a lecture delivered 1933.
14 J. Tamburrini, 'Play and intellectual development', *Paedaogica Europaea*, Vol. 9, No. 1, 1974, pp. 57–8.
15 K. Sylva, C. Roy and M. Painter, *Child Watching at Playgroup and Nursery School*, Grant McIntyre, London, 1980.
16 N.A. Chomsky, *Reflections on Language*, Temple Smith, London, 1976.
17 J. Macnamara, 'Cognitive basis of language learning in infants', *Psychological Review*, Vol. 7, No. 9, 1972, pp. 1–13.
18 M. Donaldson, 'Learning language', in M. Robert and J. Tamburrini (eds.), *Child Development 0–5*, Holmes McDougall, Edinburgh, 1981.
19 J. Tough, *Listening to Children Talking*, Ward Lock, London, 1976.
20 M. Almy, 'Spontaneous play: an avenue for intellectual development', *Bulletin of the Institute of Child Study*, Vol. 28, No. 2, 1966, p. 2.
21 B. Tizard, 'Play: the child's way of learning', in B. Tizard and D. Harvey (eds.), *The Biology of Play*, Heinemann, London, 1977.
22 Sylva, Roy and Painter, op. cit. (note 15).
23 V. Thomas, 'Children's use of language in the nursery', *Educational Research*, Vol. 15, No. 3, 1973, pp. 209–16.
24 D. Woods, L. McMahan and Y. Cranstoun, *Working with Under-Fives*, Grant McIntyre, London, 1980.
25 Sylva, Roy and Painter, op. cit. (note 15).
26 B. Tizard, 'Language at home and at school', in C.B. Cazden (ed.), *Language and Early Childhood Education*, US National Association for Young Children, Washington DC, 1979.

27 B. Tizard and M. Hughes, *Young Children Learning*, Fontana, London, 1984.
28 B. Robson, 'Encouraging interaction between staff and children in pre-school units', in M.M. Clark (ed.) '*Special Educational Needs and Children under Five*,' Educational Review, Occasional Publications 9, Faculty of Education, University of Birmingham, 1983.
29 Sylva, Roy and Painter, op. cit. (note 15).
30 L.G. Katz, 'Fostering communicative competence in young children', in M.M. Clark (ed.), 'Helping Communication in Early Education', *Educational Review*, Occasional Publications 11, Faculty of Education, University of Birmingham, 1985.
31 M. Maclure and P. French, 'A comparison of talk at home and at school', in G. Wells (ed.), *Learning through Interaction*, Cambridge University Press, 1981.
32 Dorset County Council, *Mathematics with the Youngest Children*, Dorchester, 1984.
33 E. Choat, *Children's Acquisition of Mathematics*, NFER, Slough, 1978.
34 M. Hughes, 'What is difficult about learning arithmetic', in M. Donaldson (ed.), *Early Childhood Development and Education*, Blackwell, Oxford, 1983.
35 J. Piaget, *Play, Dreams and Imitation in Childhood*, Norton, New York, 1951.
36 K. Jameson, *Pre-School and Infant Art*, Studio Vista, London, 1974.
37 Piaget, op. cit. (note 35).
38 M. Clay, *What Did I Write?*, Heinemann, London, 1975.
39 Schools Council, *The Practical Curriculum* (Working Paper 70), Methuen, London, 1981.
40 D.B. Stendler, 'Critical periods in socialisation and overdependency', *Child Development*, Vol. 23, 1952, pp. 3–13.
41 J. and E. Newson, *Four Years Old in an Urban Community*, Allen & Unwin, London, 1968.
42 E. Erikson, *Childhood and Society*, Penguin, Harmondsworth, 1963.
43 L. Webb, *Purpose and Practice in Nursery Education*, Blackwell, Oxford, 1974.
44 Blatchford, Battle and Mays, op. cit. (note 5).
45 Z. Rubin, 'The skills of friendship', in M. Donaldson (ed.), *Early Childhood Development and Education*, Blackwell, Oxford, 1983.
46 M. Hohmann, B. Banet and D. Weikart, *Young Children in Action*, High Scope Press, Ypsilanti, Mich., 1979.
47 J. Piaget and B. Inhelder, *The Child's Conception of Space*, Routledge & Kegan Paul, London, 1956.
48 H. Borke, 'Piaget's mountains revisited: changes in the egocentric landscape', in M. Donaldson (ed.), *Early Childhood Development and Education*, Blackwell, Oxford, 1983.
49 J. Piaget, *The Child's Conception of Number*, Routledge & Kegan Paul, London, 1952.
50 J. McGarrigle and M. Donaldson, 'Conservation accidents', *Cognition*, Vol. 3, 1974, pp. 341–50.
51 M. Donaldson, *Children's Minds*, Fontana, London, 1978.
52 Vygotsky, op. cit. (note 13).
53 Woods, McMahan and Cranstoun, op. cit. (note 24).
54 Sylva, Roy and Painter, op. cit. (note 15).

55 B. Robson, 'Encouraging interaction between staff and children with communication problems in pre-school', in M.M. Clark (ed.), *Special Educational Needs and Children Under Five*, Educational Review Occasional Papers No. 9, 1983.

56 Hughes, op. cit. (note 34).

57 Brierley, op. cit. (note 4).

58 M.D. Sheridan, *From Birth to Five Years: Children's Development Progress*, NFER/Nelson, Slough, 1983 (reprint).

59 D.L. Gallahue, *Motor Development and Movement Experience for Young Children*, Wiley, New York, 1976.

60 M.G. Cooper, 'Observational studies in nursery school', Ph.D. thesis, Durham University, 1977. C. Hutt, *Males and Females*, Penguin, Harmondsworth, 1972. P. Wetton, 'Some observations of interest in locomotor and gross motor activities in the nursery school', *Physical Education Review*, Vol. 6, No. 2, 1983, p. 12429.

61 E. Erikson, 'Growth and crisis in the healthy personality', *Psychological Issues*, Vol. 1, 1959, p. 1.

62 J. Piaget, *The Moral Judgement of the Child*, Routledge & Kegan Paul, London, 1932.

3

PLANNING WITH AND FOR THE FAMILY

It is difficult to consider nursery education without looking at the child in the context of his family. As we have seen, the notion of parents being informed about and involved in their child's education is not new. Since Plowden suggested that parent interest was the most important factor in educational attainment, other government statements have reflected this view. In 1975 the Bullock Report, essentially concerned with reading and language development, recommended close parental involvement to facilitate progress during the early years.[1]

The Court Report in 1976 stated that 'services for the very young child must not be allowed to become over-professionalized: instead they should seek to work through the family, encouraging its strengths and helping its shortcomings. There is overwhelming evidence that measures that do not involve parents achieve only short-term gains.'[2] The Warnock Committee added its voice in 1978: 'In the earliest years, parents rather than teachers should be regarded wherever possible as the main educators of their children.'[3] Although such policy statements have given a constant message for the past twenty years, however, there has been little attempt until recently by central government to implement these recommendations.

In this chapter we shall argue that consideration of the child within the family is essential for any nursery that acknowledges the importance of the home, the need for continuity of learning and the nursery teacher's responsibility toward families in the community. The term 'parental involvement' is used in a variety of contexts and to cover a variety of purposes. A brief look at nurseries that claim to work with parents soon discloses a range of practices. Some establishments cautiously acknowledge that parents have a right of access but little more. Others are proud of the daily presence of a number of parents tackling different tasks with children during the nursery day; when one looks more closely, though, it is often difficult to see any planning or purpose to this involvement, other than the principle that 'we can always use an extra pair of hands'. Yet other nurseries may have a detailed written policy for parents; a stack of paperwork may be generated to keep parents informed, but the spirit of working together is not present.

If working to promote parental involvement is to be more than just a teaching fashion, the nursery teacher must be clear about her intentions and methods. Below we consider some broad approaches to working with parents. Some nurseries will feel able to develop work in only one or two areas, but teachers should keep informed and be open-minded about other possibilities.

INITIAL EXCHANGE OF INFORMATION

Looking at the role of parents and governing bodies, the Taylor Report emphasized that 'Every parent has a right to expect a school's teachers to recognize his status in the education of his child by the practical arrangements they make to communicate with him and the spirit in which they accept his interest.'[4] The 1980 Education Act followed by reinforcing parents' rights to certain information about their child's school. However, no legislation is likely to identify with sensitivity the questions that concern parents before they send their child to a nursery. These may include the worry of how their child will adapt to a new regime and environment; what will be expected of the child; how he will get on with other children; and what he will learn that will be of assistance to him in his future schooling.

The nursery teacher must always be aware of the starting-point of the parent, especially the parent of a first child who will need to learn so much about this next step in his life. It may be necessary to stress that all provision for under-fives is voluntary. This is obvious to the professional but not always recognized by the new parent, who may feel under pressure to school her child when her own preference is to have him at home a little longer.

If parents are to make an informed choice about sending their child to a nursery they must know what is available. Attendance at baby groups or mother-and-toddler groups may have allowed some mothers to share their knowledge about local provision, although the NFER study on transition to pre-school found that mother-and-toddler groups were not necessarily very popular with parents. The report suggests that friends and relatives were the greatest source of information, and only 14 per cent of parents had heard of nurseries through visits to clinics, doctors and libraries.[5]

While in some areas there is very little provision for families with under-fives, in others the range of opportunities can itself be confusing and off-putting for parents. Some local authorities have provided useful handbooks of services for young families; others have set up advice centres such as the one staffed by psychologists in two Islington health centres or the parent advice service operated weekly in Hartlepool. The picture is patchy, with the need not only for additional provision in some areas but for a more concerted effort to inform parents with babies and toddlers about all the facilities that exist for children up to five. Parents then need to be encouraged to view these provisions for themselves to decide what is most appropriate for their child. Some parents may only have one provision available, however, and a nursery class may be strictly required to receive children only from a clearly defined catchment area.

From the time that the child is registered there should be opportunities for parents to gain more specific information about the nursery. Two-thirds of the parents interviewed in the transition study indicated that they wanted to meet the nursery staff.[6] Parents are also likely to be eager to see the facilities that their children will be using, and some will want information about the nursery curriculum. The period before the child starts at the nursery can be important for getting to know about all these aspects of provision, and some informal parent groups can provide a useful forum for meeting staff in a relaxed atmosphere and generally becoming familiar with the nursery setting. A school brochure will enable parents to read information at home and show it to their friends and neighbours. Tizard suggests that the best way of finding out what to put in a school brochure is to ask established parents what they would have liked to see included.[7] In the main, written information is probably most useful when it deals with factual matters such as names and roles of staff and governors, and information about routines such as daily dinner arrangements and provision for health inspection. It would be a mistake to rely on a brochure as a totally effective way of communication; at best it is helpful to have a written statement of what has already been discussed in a small group meeting with parents.

Staffing and the nursery environment and routines are relatively easy to communicate, but the nursery curriculum poses a greater challenge. This curriculum is not easy to explain to parents, who tend to think in terms of the subject-based, examination-oriented schoolwork that they last remember.

The way the nursery expresses its purposes and practices depends on the catchment area and on the understanding of parents. There is a range of educational material for parents through books, articles, Open University study units and television and radio programmes; some parents will have taken every opportunity to use this information and will arrive at the nursery with their child, conversant with many aspects of child development and learning. Other parents, equally aspiring for their children, may not be so aware or may hold different views. Tizard suggested that in most middle-class schools the parents were familiar with many educational terms and thus could more quickly grasp the reasons for specific activities: 'Parents with less previous exposure to these concepts and unfamiliar with modern theories of development and learning were at best likely to gather that the teacher believed that children in some way learned through playing with sand.'[8]

Further communication complications can arise if the nursery serves families from different cultures. Asian and West Indian families can have very different ideas about their children's upbringing and the place of play and toys in their children's education. If teachers are unaware of these views they may be in danger of enthusiastically promoting children's activities which make no sense at all to some parents. Tizard reports that 'it is not surprising that the teachers in our project from schools with a large proportion of non-indigenous parents became discouraged by failures of communication and generally abandoned attempts to run evening meetings, toy libraries or even book libraries'.[9]

There's thus a need to be very clear about the size of the communication gap before offering parents information. The better informed teachers are about the beliefs and styles of parenting from different cultures, the more sensitively they can move toward explaining how a nursery can help children.

A good example of this is the work of home–school liaison teachers involved in a Parents in Partnership project in the North. In making videos to enhance home–school dialogue, a 'pyramid approach' was used: 'that is, a situation familiar to (or aspired to by) most parents was to be used as a starting-point (for example, a child successfully reading a text). The video would then move back in time, showing the sequence of steps which lead up to the child's success.'[10]

There is a general view that the more parents know about the methods and content of education, the better they are able to support their child's learning. However, it appears that there is still a great deal of work to do in this area. Recent studies reveal that most parents see nursery education as primarily fostering social development.[11] Although social development is important, this view implies a need for nursery staff to be more explicit about other aspects of their work and to couch their explanations in terms parents can understand. The pyramid approach seems an effective way of linking nursery activity to parents' long-term aspirations for their children.

Much emphasis has been placed on how schools can help and support parents. Much less attention has been given to how the parent can assist the professional. Yet the amount of information that every parent has about her child is likely to be unmatched. Whatever the home circumstances or quality of relationship that exists, parents know about their child as an individual – his fears and excitements, his favourite playthings, his stamina and emotional strengths and weaknesses. They will also be aware of how their young child spends his time at home.

Young and McGeeney have described the work that they tackled post-Plowden to encourage meetings, discussions with parents and home visits. Teachers commented on their increased awareness of their children's home lives: 'When I look at them now I think of all the things I know about them and realize just what some of them have to put up with.'[12] Such a comment suggests that teachers saw the benefits of acquiring information about their children's home lives in helping to sensitize them to the difficulties that children and parents experience, thus making the teachers more sympathetic in their school provision. More recently, however, studies have revealed more positive reasons for teachers becoming better informed, by stressing the wealth of learning that takes place in the home. Wells's study, which represented all social groups, reported on the rich use of language at home by all children.[13]

Tizard and Hughes's study was less representative but supported this view.[14] The authors outlined why they considered the child's learning at home to be so productive, suggesting that a wide range of activities takes place in or around the home which provides the young child with a range of information, particularly about the roles of adults. Tizard and Hughes also indicate that small family size means the likelihood of a small number of children sharing the adults' time, and the time that is shared is linked to common past and present experiences. Furthermore, any learning for the child is likely to be within the context of an everyday experience involving household routines of washing-up, bedmaking and laying the table. The study argues that the close relationship between mother and child can be a positive factor in promoting the child's learning, more particularly the parent's personal aspirations for her child.

The study by Tizard and Hughes admittedly has a suggestion of the idealized home setting. Many readers will question how far this setting was affected by the presence of the researcher and whether the findings would have been the same had the study been across a wider social stratum or included boys. Despite this, the factors mentioned are very persuasive in fostering early learning. The implications are also a healthy antidote to the more usual picture of inadequate homes which are learning deserts. If we are persuaded of the learning that takes place at home, the next question is how the nursery practitioner can learn more about what happens to draw on this experience.

Whatever the level of working with parents, a welcoming atmosphere in the nursery and a friendly and open manner during home visiting will make for good, trusting relationships. However, as Tizard points out:

> although friendly relationships may make it easier to work with parents, they won't in themselves achieve the aims of parental involvement programmes. For the teacher who wants parents to understand what she is trying to achieve, to provide her with the kind of back-up she wants and to exchange views and information with her, informal contacts are not enough.[15]

Even at the level of offering and receiving information from parents, difficulties emerge through lack of resources. Teachers can tackle only what is possible. One sensible approach may be for each member of the nursery team to be allowed a 'case-load' of families. It is then the particular responsibility of that member of staff to relate to those parents and to develop a home profile which can then be used as a basis for developing further conversation and learning in the nursery. If a parent is aware that she has a particular adult as a first point of contact this can make it easier to share information about her child.

Suggested action

Inform parents of available local facilities

- Find out about the range of statutory and voluntary provision for young families in the locality; keep a list of these to offer nursery parents with younger babies and toddlers, and ensure that these groups have information about the nursery to offer to their parents.
- Familiarize yourself with local playgroups; it helps if you can refer a parent to a local group if your nursery admission limit has been reached.
- Plan a weekend presentation when the nursery and other under-fives agencies publicize the range of facilities available for young families. This event needs to be publicized in the local press and on local radio.

- Arrange for nursery brochures, posters and displays of nursery work to be seen in local libraries, doctors' surgeries and supermarkets.

Plan a positive reception for parents at registration

The first impression of the nursery that a parent and child receive is crucial.

- Make it nursery policy that all prospective parents and children are warmly received and, if at all possible, shown around the nursery at that time. If this proves difficult, a convenient time should be arranged for the parent and child to return. Overcome a language problem by inviting a parent who speaks the language to accompany you with the new parent.
- Offer tangible evidence to the child that he will be coming to the nursery; e.g. provide a simple certificate to confirm the child's proposed date of entry to the nursery. The certificate can have a suitable nursery motif, a space for the child's name and attractive lettering stating that 'We look forward to you coming to our nursery.' Offer a nursery badge or sticker.
- Make the first visit brief but assure the parent that it will be one of many.
- Aim to offer some written information before the parent leaves. This may be the nursery brochure or a paper showing the proposed sequence of events leading up to the child's admission to the nursery; e.g. availability of weekly parent/toddler group; details of an introductory home visit to be paid by the teacher; details and dates of admission procedures for new children.

Plan the nursery brochure

- Make the nursery brochure attractive and concise, using clear print and relevant illustrations.
- Make the information directly applicable to new parents; it may be preferable to have a series of brief documents rather than try to include too much information in one booklet.
- If there is more than one document, make it clear to parents just what is available, e.g. booklets on the value of various aspects of play, on ways in which parents can help children at home.
- Include a plan of the nursery in the brochure, showing the location of various activities, the parents' room and toilets.
- Provide the information in different languages where necessary.

Local community leaders or parents could help with translations and offer advice on suitable format and illustrations.

Make personal contact with parents

- Arrange some weekly gatherings of new parents and children before they start at the nursery. The children may play alongside their parents or occasionally play in an adjoining nursery room. Parents can be given a range of information about the nursery and child management; they can see the nursery in session and can share information with other parents. Childminders should be invited to these daytime meetings if both parents are working; where most families are out all day it may be preferable to hold the meetings in the evening, having enlisted the support of established nursery parents to volunteer as baby-minders. The use of video film in the evening can be a good way of showing a nursery session.
- Arrange at least one semi-social gathering for new parents and teachers to meet over coffee, tea and cake after school or cheese and wine. This should provide an opportunity for the teachers to be seen as people; volunteer parents or nursery-assistant students could supervise children in an adjoining crèche.
- Some parents may feel more relaxed making initial contact on their home territory. The teacher might notify her intention to visit by sending the child a special nursery postcard. The aim of the visit should be to confirm arrangements for the child to start at the nursery and to reassure the parent and child if they have particular anxieties. A volunteer interpreter should accompany the teacher where there may be a language barrier.

Explain the nursery curriculum

- Offer nursery pamphlets which help to explain the educational value of different activities. Those are more likely to be read if they are given to parents after an informal meeting or discussion on that particular activity.
- Develop a parents' library with a range of books on child development and early childhood curriculum; these might be purchased from a parents' fund which parents could organize themselves. Multi-ethnic centres can advise on literature available for parents of different cultures.
- Invite the local infant head teacher (or heads, in the case of a nursery school feeding a number of infant schools) to meetings

with parents. In an informal setting the infant staff can help parents to be aware that activity learning continues in the main school.

Learn from parents

- Create opportunities to listen. Before starting at the nursery, parents should be asked to share what they know about their child with a positive emphasis. Tailor this opportunity to the particular catchment area. It may take place in the home or the nursery and may involve parents responding to a questionnaire or informally chatting to the teacher.
- Note home events. Offer a specific invitation for parents regularly to share any items of family interest which may have affected their child, e.g. death of a pet, dad getting a new job. This information may be conveyed casually, or there may be a regular time when each member of staff may be available to her small group of parents. A cup of tea after school with a volunteer older mum keeping an eye on the children will enable a more leisurely discussion between teacher and parents.

WORKING TOGETHER

The child's entry to the nursery and subsequent pattern of relationships with parents has potential for establishing sound parental attitudes towards education, a growing appreciation of how their young child learns and the opportunity to keep in touch with this learning. Parents' understanding and support should in turn help the nursery teacher in her professional role. Any moves towards parents and teachers working as partners requires regular close communication, which in itself needs a commitment from both parties. Initially there seems to be a need for the nursery team to have considered how the new child can be helped to adjust to the nursery and the respective roles that teacher and parent will play in this process. The picture that emerges from studies, however, is that the settling in is often an uncertain time. Tizard found that 'the teacher might feel the mother should be left to settle her child on her own, yet the mother might not know how to do this and feel embarrassed or distressed because her child was clinging and unhappy'.[16] The mothers interviewed in the transition study were all invited to stay with their children initially, but generally felt that this might not be seriously meant. One mother said: 'I didn't stay. I think [a member of staff] prefers you out of the way so she can get on with things.' It seems that most new children settled within a few weeks, but this might be less left to chance. Any policy regarding transition must of course be left open to interpret individual needs, but parents might feel happier if they had a clearer role to play.[17]

Opportunities for keeping in touch with parents are perhaps greater in the nursery than at any other time in a child's school life. Parents are required to come into the school at least twice a day to deliver and collect their children. A staggered daily entry often provides the chance to have a word with the member of staff, and the children's own insistence that parents see any new school pet or look at their painting when displayed makes it easier for the more reticent parent to enter the nursery. When parents work and employ childminders, contact is more difficult. Parents of under-fives are in any case often under pressure, and the daily contact with the nursery may be in the company of a toddler and a baby, both requiring supervision. Early parenthood, as we saw in Chapter 1, is likely to be a time of life for young adults when relationships are relatively new and money is short. Whatever their circumstances, many nursery parents will be quite new to their role *vis-à-vis* the school and so may be not sure what to expect. For all these reasons parents may not have the time, energy or courage to ask questions or to take the initiative in becoming more actively informed about nursery developments. This points to the need for nursery staff to plan ways of keeping their parents in touch. To succeed in this, they must be sensitive to what parents want. One nursery invited parents to an open evening shortly after the children had started school. Only 50 per cent responded, and those who went indicated that they did so to be supportive to the staff rather than because they saw the occasion as useful.[18]

Bearing in mind the busy lives most parents lead, it is sensible to provide them with as much helpful information as possible without requiring them to attend a special occasion. Attractive notice-boards and handouts have their place, while an informal weekly briefing about certain activities can take place with parents towards the end of the nursery session during the children's story-time.

Apart from gaining information about the nursery regime, every parent has a right to know how her child is succeeding. This 'right' is not recognized or acted upon by many parents. Studies show that parents are usually anxious to be reassured that their child is happy and physically cared for, but they rarely ask additional questions.[19] However, when asked specifically whether they had sufficient information, one group of parents emphasized that they would have liked to know more about their child's progress.[20] Teachers generally respond to requests for information rather than volunteer it. Understandably, because of the problems of time, priority is given to reassuring expressed anxieties. However, if parents are to appreciate the value of nursery education and have the opportunity of sharing an informed view of the progress of their child there is a need for more specific information. Sylva and Moore's study on record-keeping in nurseries revealed that individual children's records are rarely used as an aid to discussion with parents. In 1983 this study of 125 local authorities reported that 81 per cent of the authorities show records to parents only 'rarely' or 'occasionally': 'It seems safe to conclude that records are used more for "working" purposes than for communication, perhaps missing out on a valuable means of working in partnership with parents.'[21]

Suggested action

Settling the child

- Provide a simple illustrated booklet for parents, outlining common forms of behaviour expected from new entrants with guidance for parent/teacher action (see Appendix 1).
- Take every opportunity to relate to the new parent and child and help them to manage the initial separation. You may do this by:
  - joining them at the child's chosen activity and working with them (during this time the teacher can listen to and take part in the shared experiences of parent and child and use them with the child after the parent has left);
  - encouraging the parent to stay if the child still needs her;
  - involving the parent in some activity as a step towards separation; e.g. simple tasks such as cutting paper or mixing paints will allow the parent to observe how her child copes with other children and becomes involved without her;
  - suggesting when you think it is appropriate for the parent to leave if the parent is reluctant to take the decision;
  - giving the parent a detailed account of how her child has spent his time since she left him for the session.

Share information through notices and displays

- The notice-board should be conveniently placed for parents to see when waiting for their children. Regular spaces for particular information and clear graphics will help parents to skim quickly for information; e.g. a space for social and fund-raising events, routine information on times and dates of opening and names and photographs of staff, details of community facilities for young families. This information should look attractive and be changed regularly to encourage parents to make use of it.

- The school brochure will give a flavour of the nursery. More detailed information can be gained by parents receiving half-termly curriculum plans from the teacher. These can include details of proposed outings, new rhymes and jingles to be introduced and proposed cookery activities.
- A small display of older children's representations in painting, drawing or construction can be used to demonstrate the skills and concepts involved; e.g. 'Joe (3 years, 11 months) made this model of his dad's new car. He had to learn to choose the materials he needed, making sure that they were the right shape and size. He learned how to apply glue and stick one surface to another. He controlled scissors to cut the shapes for the wheels. Joe concentrated for twelve minutes on his work and used the following words to describe his model: "fast", "zoomy", "zippy", "brakes", "wheels", "petrol".'
- A display of new apparatus or equipment purchased can be accompanied by a brief explanation of its learning potential.

Make personal contacts

- Regular informal discussions/workshops will work best for a group of about eight parents. The teacher who is 'responsible' for these parents gives a talk, shows equipment or uses a video to demonstrate the value of an activity and the level of development of the children involved. Over a cup of tea parents and teacher can discuss how the learning in this activity can be followed up at home; e.g. visual memory – the child can be asked to remember one or two items that the parent must buy when they go shopping; what items does he remember best?
- Make individual contact. During the first term ensure that you have spoken with each new parent to check that they are clear about the routines and activities in the nursery. The amount and level of understanding required to satisfy each parent will differ and will require a flexible response from you.

SERVICES AND SUPPORT FOR YOUNG FAMILIES

If the nursery teacher recognizes the strong link between the quality of family life and the child's well-being and progress, there must be concern to support parents in their work. The job of parenting is taxing and stressful in today's climate, and many young parents want the very best for their children but feel ill-equipped to provide it. In these cases, as well as considering parents as educators there should be some means of supporting them as people and helping them to enjoy their children. Pre-school support services vary from area to area; there are some excellent facilities available, but too often the picture is patchy and uncoordinated, with statutory and voluntary services unaware of each other's roles. In the meantime the nursery can be in a key position to receive family concerns. Regular daily contact with parents offers teachers a unique opportunity to keep in touch with problems and in particular to monitor how family life is affecting the child.

However, the dilemma for the teacher comes from lack of time and resources to offer adequate support, while recognizing that parents may use the nursery as the first point of contact for help and advice. There is no satisfactory answer to this, but the nurseries that are seen as family supporters are likely to give priority to four factors: (1) having open access to the nursery; (2) recognizing the need for some home contacts; (3) working closely with other agencies involved with young families; and (4) recognizing that parents can help one another.

In nursery centres that were operating successfully with parents the main ingredients appeared to be that parents felt they were welcome.[22] For, although many nurseries consider that they do encourage parents to visit freely, this is not always the parents' perception. Some teachers still feel uneasy about the constant presence of parents in the nursery, which can be regarded as a distraction from their work with children. Even if the presence is accepted, attitudes can appear patronizing and of the all-knowing professional bestowing advice. How initial and in-service education can help teachers to view their role in relation to adults as well as children will be discussed later (Chapter 6). Certainly interpersonal skills of tact, discretion and genuine sympathy with parents are a prerequisite of the job.

While some parents will just be receptive to facilities offered, others will want to contribute actively and to take some responsibility. Such parents can often provide a range of skills to enhance the nursery.

It is one thing to encourage parents to see the nursery as a warm and welcoming environment, but the problem of making it possible for them to have immediate access to teachers who have no non-contact time is a real one. In some catchment areas parents will appreciate that the teacher is available for them at the end of each day or by appointment; in other areas, apart from making local authorities aware of the urgent need to have extra staffing resources, it is glib to suggest that there is any alternative other than the teacher weighing up the priority of each call for help and suffering the usual pangs of role conflict.

Some parents are rarely seen, because of working commitments or physical or mental illness; others may deliver or collect their child but be unable to reveal anything of themselves in an institutionalized setting, however inviting. The benefits of home visiting to develop the parent's educative role are considered later. Here we suggest that there is a place for the nursery to extend the hand of friendship to those parents who are not seen on nursery premises. Visited at home, on their own 'territory', parents are often more at ease and more open about their own difficulties and in questioning and criticizing the nursery regime. Where home–school liaison teachers have been employed in certain authorities their visits have revealed that, 'as well as informing and advising parents, feedback from home visits helped the school identify the messages it frequently failed to put across effectively to parents'.[23]

Another important role for a home visitor may be to introduce and support parents in visiting the community facilities offered by a nursery. The Haringey Pre-School Centre exists in an area catering for around twenty different ethnic groups. Here home visitors are employed to forge a link with the family and to help them take advantage of the facilities provided. This may involve encouraging a reticent mother to make contact with other mothers at the centre, or befriending a family and helping them cope with the practicalities of life such as form-filling.[24]

In many nurseries there is no additional staffing for home visiting, so teachers must weigh up the need against other priorities. Some teachers see a home-visiting role as crucial to their work, but this is likely to be in an educational context. Nevertheless, a planned visit to welcome a new baby, visit a sick mother or to offer transport to the nursery for a child whose attendance is poor may pay dividends for future working relationships.

A nursery aiming to offer comprehensive support to young families cannot afford to operate in isolation. It needs to be aware of what other support agencies exist and to work closely with these agencies. Bradley argues strongly for the co-ordination of services for young children. He suggests that policies since the war, such as the contraction in day nursery provision and similar restrictions on nursery education in the 1960s, have been counter-productive for families. It is essential for agencies to ensure that they make the most of what services are available; expensive buildings need to be used imaginatively, given changing population trends and the need for a flexible provision. The focus on the whole child means that no one service is capable of meeting all the needs of the young family.[25]

Where children have special educational needs the 1981 Education Act now legally requires local authorities to inform and liaise with other departments and with parents in diagnosing and assessing the degree of disability. Where legislation does not exist, Bradley suggests that co-ordination is most effective if senior local government officers are involved in policy-making, which can then be carried out at grass-roots level. A nursery in such an area will have the benefit of established frameworks in which to work. It may be that there is a local authority forum for services for young children which is attended by representatives of both statutory and voluntary bodies dealing with young families. Advisers with responsibility for this age group may convene local meetings of workers from the different agencies, allowing for the exchange of information and the planning of joint initiatives.

In areas where there is no lead from the top, the practitioners have to take the initiative. Nursery teachers may need information from health visitors, paediatricians, educational psychologists and speech therapists: they also have useful information to pass on. Nurseries also need access to these agencies. A teacher may not see her role as being a marriage guidance counsellor or an expert on obtaining family benefits. She should, however, be able to refer families in need to appropriate sources of advice and information.

Links with statutory agencies may be obvious but the role of voluntary associations is also crucial. Volunteers are in a special position to help families. In describing Home Start, a scheme which introduces volunteer home visitors to families, the role was described as one of 'caring, friendship, mothering and nurturing. Unlike professionals, volunteers are more inclined to be person-orientated rather than problem-orientated . . . It is a non-threatening role where the mother may identify with the volunteer who herself is not perfect and may share her own fears and triumphs with the family.'[26]

The volunteer can therefore provide a service and offer time in a way that is difficult for a statutory worker with a large case-load. According to Sheila Wolfendale: 'the essence of many of these ventures is the two-way or reciprocal process – that a scheme can only be successful, if it has an inbuilt requisite, the active contribution and participation of the parent'.[27]

It is increasingly realized that parents will retain their dignity and hold on life if they can take an active part in helping themselves. The pre-school playgroup movement is a good example of parents' self-help initially in providing facilities for their young children when nursery places were not available. The vitality of this movement today indicates the need it has met in the community for adults to join together and become involved in their pre-school children's development. The existence of playgroups in no way invalidates the case for nursery education; these two provisions, both voluntary and state-funded, could and should complement each other. Ideally parents should have choice of placement for their child – where this does not exist, close collaboration should ensure that the best possible use is made of whatever provision is there and that professionals and volunteers learn from one another.

An Australian study on postnatal depression questioned young women about what type of help they had found most effective. The mothers responded that by far the most important was sympathy, reassurance, and encouragement received, whilst the least helpful was medication.[28] In extreme cases time and care offered to a young parent and her family may avoid the children being taken into care later. Nurseries need to be aware of the resource many of their parents may provide as volunteer helpers to support particular families. Such groups as Home Start and PPA have institutionalized the support they offer. At a local level nurseries can offer a great deal just by putting people in touch with one another.

Suggested action

Encourage open access in the nursery

- Have bright signs welcoming parents into the nursery.
- Find a space for parents. An attractive room is ideal, but a space in the foyer with easy chairs and magazines at least acknowledges that parents have an area for themselves.
- Offer simple services for parents, e.g. a library of knitting patterns, or a scheme for exchanging paperbacks or magazines (this is particularly welcome for parents from different ethnic groups who may exchange their own literature).
- Offer the facilities of a toy library run regularly by volunteers.
- Provide facilities for toddlers and ask a parent to be responsible for seeing that equipment is put out and tidied away at the end of a session.

- Organize social occasions, sending personal invitations to every family; e.g. a supper prepared in turn by parents of different cultures: a family barbecue.
- Develop a drop-in centre. According to room available this may have to be a planned weekly occasion using space which is multi-purpose, or a regular provision in a permanent room. Facilities again may vary according to what is practically possible. Parents may call in with babies and toddlers once weekly for a cup of coffee, or they may use the centre for making snack lunches, ask for it to be open during holiday periods and develop a forum for discussion on issues affecting young families. When possible a member of staff should regularly visit the centre, establishing the link with the nursery. Give new parents invitation cards (illustrated by a child and written in the mother tongue), welcoming them to the centre. The new parent may also be linked with an established parent, who will introduce her to the centre and see that she makes contact with other parents.

Extend links into the home

- Arrange to receive a list of new births in the locality. Send a nursery representative on a brief home visit with a congratulations card (design your own card using children's artwork and use local authority printing facilities) and details of any pram club or new parents' support group in the area.
- In an area where parents work and access to the nursery is not easy, a termly home visit by the teacher may be a way of keeping home and nursery in touch.
- Send all parents a news-sheet giving information about any events relevant for young families.

Liaise with statutory and voluntary bodies

- Know what is available. Systematically gather information about the agencies that are available locally to help young families. Some local authorities publish handbooks offering this information; alternatively the local citizens' advice bureau should be helpful. Using this information, aim to meet a representative of each agency over a period of time to get to know more about the resources each can offer. Ask how the nursery could help for these resources to be better used in the community.

- Maintain the links:
  - Plan termly catchment meetings with representatives of all agencies working with young children and toddlers, together with local headteachers of infant and first schools. Benefits will include people getting to know each other and sharing views on matters of common concern, e.g. early childhood management, diet, support for families under stress.
  - Plan regular working lunches with the local health visitor, school nurse, social worker and speech therapist. Make this an opportunity for each in turn to raise some issue of concern or use the time to collect information about certain families and strategies of support being offered.
  - Arrange for the health visitor to spend time in the nursery regularly. Where no home visiting takes place from the nursery, the health visitor can provide the link with the home.

- Use the expertise and resources from other agencies:
  - Plan for adult education classes for parents during nursery hours either in the building or located nearby.
  - Persuade the local library to provide you with a permanent resource of books which can be on loan for parents.
  - Persuade the speech therapist to work in the nursery with all the children over a period of time. In this way she can keep in touch with children who have a range of language abilities and can have early warning of children with potential difficulties.
  - Use the parents' room and staff room to develop a monthly family support service. Have access to an educational psychologist, family social worker and speech therapist on these occasions and make it possible for parents to drop in and take the initiative in asking for advice and help rather than being directed to these agencies.

- Offer support to other agencies:
  - Develop exchange visits with local playgroups, and where practical arrange to exchange pieces of equipment, e.g. jigsaw puzzles and equipment for gross motor play.
  - In some cases playgroups will appreciate a brief loan of a piece of equipment before deciding to buy it for themselves.
  - Offer simple in-service sessions for childminders and playgroup personnel.

Help parents to 'use the system'

- Keep updated lists of childminders and playgroups on the parents' notice-board, with a local road map showing their whereabouts. Keep in touch with playgroup numbers so you can advise a parent of a vacancy if on coming to register they find a long waiting-list for the nursery.
- Invite personnel to offer information to parents, e.g. a marriage guidance counsellor, or a representative from the DHSS to talk about applications for family benefits.
- Give practical help to a group of parents who are prepared to run a holiday play scheme for their children.
- Encourage a baby-sitting service for evenings and short periods of time during school holidays.
- Sow seeds and give encouragement to a variety of parental self-help schemes, e.g. a second-hand clothes shop, arrangements for holiday outings, monthly use of the parents' room as a hairdressing salon.

DEVELOPING A FULL PARTNERSHIP

So far we have dealt with less questioned aspects of working with parents. Teachers will readily accept the need for a sensitive transition from home into the nursery, for parents to be well informed about what their children are doing, and that parents have valuable information about their own children. The principle of offering support to parents is also usually acknowledged by recognizing that this must vary with the resources available. There is general recognition that parents have rights and responsibilities in which they should be supported. However, if we accept Warnock's recommendations (see page 14) as being relevant to all parents and children, a particular approach to working with parents becomes clear. All the contact, information and support given is ultimately in the recognition of the parent's own central role as the child's educator. The suggestions for working given so far will all assist the development of a well-informed and cared-for parent body, but further work is needed to strengthen parents' ability to educate.

Before this must come the teacher's own conviction for the work. Tizard suggested in her study that nursery and infant teachers were limited in how they were prepared to work with parents by their view of professionalism, which meant that their work should not be discussed or evaluated by laymen. She argues that the notion of teacher professionalism needs widening. This would involve teachers seeing themselves as people with special skills and knowledge, who are able not only to use these skills with children but also to explain their work to a lay audience, thus acknowledging the educational contribution which parents can make and accepting that they may have a valid point of view on educational matters.[29] Recognition of this role goes further than the message coming from the major reports and initiatives of the 1960s and 1970s. Plowden and Bullock both acknowledged the need for parents to be better informed about school processes, but no mention was made of the parents' teaching role.

Parents are, however, a child's first teachers. The crucial nature of the earliest years of life is now generally accepted. This sensitive time for intervention coincides with the young child's attachment to his family, when he spends the bulk of his time in the family setting. Action research studies in this field support such arguments.

The Haringey project offered good evidence, although the study focused on seven-year-olds. The work showed that the organized involvement of parents in their child's reading at home could lead to noticeable attainments in the child's level of reading.[30] These gains were significantly better than those of a matched group of children who had received extra specialized help with reading in school. Since this study a number of projects such as PACT in Hackney, the Belfield Scheme in Rochdale and Booked by Dorset are realizing similar benefits of full parental involvement.

Tizard's current project concerning achievement of children in infant schools offers further support for the parental role. Successful test scores in mathematics, reading, writing and verbal reasoning, achieved by children at point of entry to infant school, were found to be closely correlated with three home factors: where the mother had achieved a reasonable level of education herself; where some form of home teaching had taken place with the mother, however informal; and where the mother had a clear idea of her educational role.[31]

When considering the effectiveness of parents working with their three- and four-year-olds the 1979 Renfrewshire study elicited the help of mothers as home teachers for their children. On the basis of thirty minutes' daily intervention, gains in IQ were made over a four-month period.[32] On a broader front the work on early language development by Wells and Tizard (see page 80) indicates the power of the home environment as the setting for early talk, the 'good teaching' that is already being done by parents of all social classes acting intuitively, and the potential for development of learning if teachers and parents work closely together.

Running concurrently with these funded research projects is a range of general local authority programmes acknowledging the central role of parents. Some of these are relatively modest, such as the Scope project in Hampshire, which uses space in a first school, the services of adult education and one home visitor to operate a Parent Education Unit.[33] Others are more generously funded, such as in Lothian where the Education Department employs fifteen home visitors resourced with educational materials to work with parents in the home.[34] Recognizing the worth of this type of work has also led to some local authorities being given grants to support work with parents and young children in specific circumstances. These include the authorities funded by central government to appoint personnel to work with ethnic minorities,[35] and the education support grant given to Dorset to fund two nursery teachers and two fully equipped vans to offer support to young families living in rural areas.[36]

Although these projects differ in organization and resourcing the principle is the same: to affect the child's learning, the parents must be involved. The long-term effects of these projects remain to be seen. But Armstrong and Brown, studying one of the earliest home intervention programmes, found that although sustained educational gains had not been maintained by the children the parents showed more awareness of and interest in their child's education than a matched group of parents who had not been visited.[37] The Lothian home visitors also found that the success of their work depended on the parents' own feelings of self-confidence. Any effective programme to help parents help their children thus requires not only offered expertise but acknowledgement of whole family needs.

Where a child suffers from some educational disability there is perhaps even greater need for the family context to be considered. The 1981 Act now makes clear the rights of parents to be involved with referral, assessment, statementing and review procedures and gives them the power of appeal to the Secretary of State in the event of any dispute regarding placements.[38] This legal recognition can only be helpful, although developing the spirit of the Act is all-important. Parents could be called upon to contribute at every stage of assessment and decision-making without these contributions being fully acknowledged in the outcomes. Parents need to see that their knowledge and views do affect the decisions about their child.

There are various projects with parents and professionals working together genuinely using parental expertise. The Portage home teaching model has been in existence since the 1970s, used originally in Wisconsin and now extensively in Britain.[39] The project enables home teachers drawn from a variety of professions and lay people to support the parent in teaching her own child specific skills with the aid of regular visits; work is based on a developmental checklist and activity chart. More recently, video courses have been used in a Dublin school. The video cassettes are accompanied by a handbook and suggest activities for parents to carry out with their children at home.[40] In recognition of the special information that parents have concerning their children, Wolfendale has pioneered the compilation of parental profiles and developmental checklists of their children.[41] All these approaches used in the special-needs field are equally useful for other families.

However exciting a scheme that is put forward, the parent has to be aware of its worth and to recognize her own significance in joining in with it. The parents interviewed in the 1981 Tizard study, with the exception of the middle-class group, tended to see their major role as instilling discipline and good manners in their children rather than as developing play or reading stories, which were viewed as important by the teachers. Tizard reports that between two-thirds and three-quarters of the parents concentrated on developing 'three Rs' skills with their children, often without the knowledge of the teacher.[42]

Although their view of developing early learning may differ from that of the teacher, studies reveal that parents are generally keen to help their children. Smith (1980) reports that more than half the parents in her study would have liked to play a larger part in their child's group and to share his experience more closely: 'this is the strongest possible indication of the waste of interest on the part of parents – interest in their children's experience and development that could have been built on for both parent and child'.[43]

This 'waste of interest' is likely to occur where teachers have a low expectation of what parents are prepared to do. In the 1981 study, half the nursery teachers in Tizard's sample considered that parents were too stressed and tired to make any contribution to their children's education. In her later study of thirty-one infant teachers in inner London, a number had a low perception of the interest and involvement parents would have in their children's education once they started school. Twenty-nine per cent of these teachers anticipated that none or very few of their parents would do anything to help their child. A further 16 per cent felt unable to suggest whether there would be any involvement. This view of what would be likely to happen contrasted strongly with the parents' expressed intentions. With very few exceptions the 202 parents interviewed said they would want to continue helping their child at home once he had started school. The study has not yet investigated whether these intentions have been fulfilled.[44]

Where teachers do not have a high expectation of the parental role, there is danger of a self-fulfilling prophecy. Parents who do not have a stake in their children's early education place a heavy responsibility on the nursery or school to succeed alone.

In recent years there have been significant moves from some parents who feel they have an active part to play in their children's education. These moves include the growth of parent consumer groups such as the Advisory Centre for Education, founded in 1960, and the Confederation for the Advancement of State Education, founded in 1962. These groups are supported by only a small percentage of parents, but they represent a view that questions educational policies and practice.

A more widespread group of parents is represented through the Pre-School Playgroup Association, which exists to promote self-help play facilities for children. Where the groups run as community ventures there is genuine opportunity for parents to assume responsibility for the provision. The parents who have been so involved often expect this to continue once their child has been admitted to nursery.

Suggested action

Make parents aware of their own educational role

- Have an introductory pamphlet available for new parents, stressing the importance of their role.
- Provide a range of simple games and books for parents to use with their children at home. These may be left by a home visitor, who will first have demonstrated how to use them, or they may be part of a library in the nursery. Parents and children can choose the material together and use it with the teacher in the nursery before taking it home.
- Run a series of weekly sessions for new parents using activity sheets suggesting suitable things to do with their children at home.
- During the sessions parents can discuss the effectiveness of the activities tackled during the previous week as well as raising general issues of child management and learning.
- Indicate the range of learning opportunities available for young children; e.g. talk with parents about the learning involved in daily home routines; use video material to demonstrate sequencing

involved in dressing, making a bed, making a cup of tea, washing up.

- Offer a range of simple handouts indicating the range of activity and potential learning involved in family outings: on the beach; in the car; in the park; in the garden.

Develop parents' expertise

- When parents help in the nursery, offer models of managing children and introducing them to new experiences. It may be necessary to make these models explicit, stressing that the approach is not a teacher's prerogative but will work successfully for parents as well; e.g. avoiding confrontation; sharing a task with a child.
- Run curriculum workshops; e.g. 'story time with your child' – include ways of offering stories through pictures, reading texts and telling stories; show some visual aids to use, such as stick-, hand- and finger-puppets, a picture chart hung in the child's bedroom or a 'magic bag' in which a special book or object linked to a story can be found.
- Run workshops on child development; e.g. five one-hour sessions including topics such as 'your child is unique', 'what happens to your child between one month and five years', 'communicating with your child', 'learning with you at home'.

Make resources available for parents

- Run a weekly bookshop for parents and children. Include useful resource books for parents.
- Build up a lending library of books on child development and learning. (Parents' fund can be used for this purpose.)
- Demonstrate some simple games that parents can play with their children at home. Run workshops for parents to make some of these games for use at home. (A realistic charge may be made for materials, or costs may be met from school funds.)

Give parents responsibility for their children's learning

- Provide a 'link card' to accompany any books and games going home. Encourage parents to record their comments after using this material with their child.
- Hold a regular 'surgery' at the end of the day or in early evening, when parents can share with you any particular observed developments or delays in their child's learning and behaviour. Provide

parents with a simple record booklet in which they can jot down any observed behaviour of interest.

- Having explained nursery routines fully to new parents, ask each parent to take responsibility for explaining these routines to their own child and checking that he is conversant with them.
- Display information about and addresses for the Advisory Centre for Education, the British Association for Early Childhood Education and other organizations of interest.
- Encourage parents to plan their own reading study groups and allow them to have access to the Open University pre-school video cassettes, which can be used in each other's homes.

REFERENCES

1 Department of Education and Science (DES), *A Language for Life* (Bullock Report), HMSO, London, 1975.
2 Committee on Child Health Services, *Fit for the Future* (Court Report), HMSO, London, 1976.
3 DES, *Special Educational Needs: Report of the Committee of Enquiry into the Education of Handicapped Children and Young People, under the Chairmanship of Mrs H. M. Warnock*, HMSO, London, 1978.
4 DES, *A New Partnership for Our Schools* (Taylor Report), HMSO, London, 1977.
5 P. Blatchford, S. Battle and J. Mays, *The First Transition: Home to Pre-School*, National Foundation for Educational Research (NFER)/Nelson, Slough, 1982.
6 Ibid.
7 B. Tizard, J. Mortimore and B. Burchell, *Involving Parents in Nursery and Infant Schools*, Grant McIntyre, London, 1981.
8 Ibid.
9 Ibid.
10 F. Macleod, *Parents in Partnership: Involving Muslim Parents in their Children's Education*. Community Education Development Centre, Briton Road, Coventry CV2 4LF, 1985.
11 Blatchford, Battle and Mays. op. cit. (note 5). Tizard, Mortimore and Burchell, op. cit. (note 7).
12 M. Young and P. McGeeney, *Learning Begins at Home*, Routledge & Kegan Paul, London, 1968.
13 G. Wells, *Language Development in the Pre-School Years*, Cambridge University Press, 1984.
14 B. Tizard and M. Hughes, *Young Children Learning*, Fontana, London, 1984.
15 Tizard, Mortimore and Burchell, op. cit. (note 7).
16 Ibid.
17 Blatchford, Battle and Mays, op. cit. (note 5).
18 Ibid.

19 Ibid.
20 Tizard, Mortimore and Burchell, op. cit. (note 7).
21 K. Sylva and E. Moore, 'Record keeping in nurseries', unpublished ms., 1984.
22 E. Ferri, B. Birchall and Y. Gingell, *Combined Nursery Centres*, National Children's Bureau, London, 1981.
23 Macleod, op. cit. (note 10).
24 M. Stacey, 'Partnership in a multi-cultural pre-school centre', in *Partnership Paper 1*, National Children's Bureau, London, 1983.
25 M. Bradley, *The Co-Ordination of Services for Children Under Five*, NFER/Nelson, Slough, 1982.
26 L. Wright, 'Parents as home visitors', in *Partnership Paper 5*, National Children's Bureau, London, 1985.
27 S. Wolfendale, 'A framework for action: professionals and parents as partners', in *Partnership Paper 1*, National Children's Bureau, London, 1983.
28 'Postnatal depression: a medical or cultural problem?', *New Parent*, (Australia), June 1983.
29 Tizard, Mortimore and Burchell, op. cit. (note 7).
30 B. Tizard, W. N. Schofield and J. Hewison, 'Collaboration between teachers and parents in assisting children's reading', *British Journal of Educational Psychology*, Vol. 52, 1982, pp. 1–15.
31 P. Blatchford, J. Burke, C. Farquhar, I. Plewis and B. Tizard, 'Educational achievement in the infant school: the influence of ethnic origin, gender and home on entry skills', *Educational Research*, Vol. 27, No. 1, 1985, p. 1.
32 M. M. Clark and W. N. Cheyne, *Studies in Pre-School Education*, Hodder & Stoughton, London, 1979.
33 L. Poulton, 'Parents as educators', in *Partnership Paper 5*, National Children's Bureau, London, 1985.
34 E. Whitham and G. Aplin, 'School-based schemes in Lothian', in G. Aplin and G. Pugh (eds.), *Perspectives on Pre-School Home Visiting*, National Children's Bureau/Community Education Development Centre, London, 1983.
35 Macleod, op. cit. (note 10).
36 Dorset County Council, *Educational Support Grant for Small Rural Primary Schools*, Dorchester, 1985.
37 G. Armstrong and F. Brown, *Five Years On*, Social Evaluation Unit, Oxford University Department of Social and Administrative Studies, 1979.
38 DES, *Young Children with Special Educational Needs*, HMSO, London, 1981.
39 R.J. Cameron, 'A problem-centred approach to family problems', in B. Daly (ed.), *Portage: The Importance of Parents*, NFER/Nelson, Slough, 1985.
40 R. McConkey, 'New approaches to parental involvements in pre-school education', in M. M. Clark (ed.), *Special Educational Needs and Children Under Five*, Educational Review Occasional Papers No. 9, 1983.
41 S. Wolfendale, 'Involving parents in assessment', in *Partnership Paper 3*, National Children's Bureau, London, 1983.
42 Tizard, Mortimore and Burchell, op. cit. (note 7).
43 T. Smith, *Parents and Pre-School*, Grant McIntyre, London, 1980.
44 Blatchford *et al.*, op. cit. (note 31).

4

MAKING IT WORK

We have looked at curriculum priorities for young children and the contribution that parents can make in the nursery. We must now consider how these desirable practices can take place. Two main aspects are important here: (1) the organization of resources, and (2) the use of these resources in a daily programme of teaching and learning. John Dewey described organization as 'nothing but getting things into connection with one another so that they work easily, flexibly and fully'.[1] Good organization requires careful preparation and planning. In this chapter we consider organization of the environment, of equipment, of the daily programme and children's learning, and the role played by the teacher in effecting learning.

ORGANIZING THE NURSERY ENVIRONMENT

The setting in which learning takes place is crucial to the quality of provision. The environment includes both inside and outside areas – furnishings, fitments and equipment. Buildings differ considerably; one teacher may find herself in a brand-new purpose-built nursery unit attached to a school, another in a mobile classroom in a remote corner of a school site, and yet another in a nursery school established in the early post-war years. Some teachers have to accommodate young children in a primary classroom offering few concessions to the developmental needs of this age group. Some of these buildings will present more opportunities than others. The purpose-built classroom may have adjoining toilets, direct access to an outside play area and fixtures at child height, but space may be limited. The mobile classroom is likely to offer the greatest challenge, while the older, separate nursery school is likely to offer greater potential for learning – extra space, small rooms and corners providing ideal areas for small groups of children – although the problem may be that of overseeing all the activity.

Despite the variety of buildings, given space and siting in a self-contained area of any school building, it is possible to develop a nursery ethos. Where decisions are made to bring in children of non-statutory school age, the best possible accommodation must be made available. The teacher has no choice about the building she inherits. It is up to her to consider very carefully the opportunities and constraints, to exploit the former and consider how she can compensate for the latter.

The outside space should be considered an integral part of the learning environment for children. Children of nursery age should have their own outside area, even if their accommodation is in a primary school. In the words of Lady Allen of Hurtwood, a pioneer in fighting for space for children:

> Children seek access to a place where they can dig in the earth, build huts and dens with timber, use real tools, experiment with fire and water, take really great risks and learn to overcome them. They want a place where they can create and destroy, where they can build their own worlds, with their own skills, at their own time, and in their own way. In our built-up towns, they never find these opportunities. They're frustrated at every turn or tidied out of existence.[2]

These comments remind us of the ideal. Nursery teachers have an obligation to enrich to the full any outside space that they have.

Nursery design affects how adults and children work. A small-scale study by Neill suggested that in a large open space adults tended to oversee a range of activities rather than become involved with specific children.[3] That same study supports previous findings by Sylva and by Smith and Connelly that it is harder for children to settle and play profitably in large open spaces and in larger groups.[4] When more space was made available in an experimental playgroup, the children increased running and chasing activity, but there was little or no change in social behaviour.

Whatever the design, the way the building is used reflects the beliefs of the adults who work there. In 1905 an inspector with the Board of Education described a nursery environment:

> Let us now follow the baby of three years through part of one day of school life. He is placed on a hard wooden bench (sometimes it is only a step of a gallery) with a desk in front of him and a window behind him, which is too high up to be instrumental in providing such amusement as watching passers-by. He often cannot reach the floor with his feet, and in many cases he has no back to lean against. He is told to fold his arms and to sit quiet. He is surrounded by a large number of other babies all under similar alarming and incomprehensible conditions.[5]

In 1979 the High Scope classroom is planned somewhat differently: 'The classroom is divided into well-defined work areas and the materials in each area are logically organized and clearly labelled, which enables the child to act independently and with as much control over the classroom environment as possible.'[6] These two examples show that room organization can either hinder or help children's learning.

An aesthetically pleasing environment is part of a nursery heritage. The arrangement of displays, furniture and soft furnishings should, however, reveal a knowledge of child development and provide a stimulus for learning. Because sensory experiences are so crucial at this stage, the environment should provide them, bearing in mind the size of an average three- or four-year-old and his physical propensities. It is for instance a waste of space to provide a chair for every child in the nursery, when children are unlikely all to be seated together except for eating purposes. Provision of a bright carpeted area is essential, however, to allow children to gather together in small groups or as a total group with the adult at certain times of the day.

An emphasis on active learning and choice of activity means a close look at circulation space in the nursery. Different activities need varying amounts of space and different floor surfaces. A building-block area needs to be sited away from circulation space (to avoid accidents). Carpet tiles both make an area comfortable for floor work and reduce noise.

When considering equipment and apparatus for the nursery there is not much research support for clear spending priorities. There is some danger of continuing to provide certain apparatus for children because of an early-years tradition without having hard evidence about how it benefits children's learning and development. In 1978 Bruner queried the traditional nursery rhetoric which praises unstructured materials and emphasizes free physical play.[7] Where studies exist, they tend to support different activities for different purposes. Pulaski investigated the degree of structure of play materials and the level of creativity of children's activity; her work suggests that less-structured materials lead to more imaginative play.[8] On the other hand, Sylva, considering intellectually challenging activity for children, argues in favour of activities with a clear goal structure such as small and large construction, art activity and jigsaws.[9]

There is scope for more work in this area. In the meantime the teacher should be clear as to the purpose and potential use of all apparatus used in the nursery. Until she has further information, theories of child development should be the basis of her spending priorities. Sensory exploration indicates the need for a range of bought-in and home-made materials and equipment which will help young children to discriminate through sight, hearing, taste, touch and smell. The physical needs encompassed in large and small motor development demand large and sturdy, indoor and outdoor equipment, and games and apparatus to develop manipulative skills. To represent their experiences in different ways children need access to art and craft materials, music and sound, building-blocks, pictures and a means of symbolic play. Having made these broad decisions, teachers then need to be sufficiently informed to select specific items of equipment which best support each of these learning needs.

With reduced or static capitation meaning less spending power, the onus is on the teacher to spend wisely. This is not easy. There is an increasingly vast amount of material on the market; teachers have limited time and are in danger of making hasty decisions influenced by an attractive photograph and a manufacturer's description in a catalogue. The alternative is to buy tried and trusted products that have been used in the nursery for some years. Teachers themselves often feel less than satisfied with this way of spending, and some clear guidelines regarding planned spending are needed.

Suggested action

The nursery building

The following factors comprise an ideal nursery environment. Check your nursery against this schedule:

- A welcoming entrance for parents and children: this may be a bright display in a humble entry porch or an elaborate foyer; but remember that it creates the first impression of the nursery for visitors and new entrants.
- Some waiting or working space for parents: a room set aside for parents is ideal, but a couple of easy chairs and some parents' books will at least ensure some degree of comfort for a waiting parent or someone working in the nursery away from children.
- A small room which will double as a withdrawal space for working with individual children, counselling parents and a staff sanctuary.
- A small servery to allow full-time children to eat their meals in the nursery even though they may be cooked in the main school kitchen: a nursery school is likely to have its own kitchen; the servery or kitchen can also be used as a cookery area for a small group of children to work with an adult.
- Storage areas should be sufficient for bulky early-years equipment including large wooden apparatus for indoor gross motor activity.

A large store with dual access to the nursery and outside area should be provided where there is no separate outside store.
- Cloakroom and lavatory facilities adjoining the classroom enable young children to collect their outdoor wear at will and also to use the lavatory unaided.
- A spacious playroom with an area of not less than eight square metres for each child: south-facing and with access to the outside play area.

The outside area

- Provide for safety. The play area must be fenced off from any vehicle entrance to the school, and any entrances must have safety hooks attached.
- Provide different levels of play; small hillocks allow children a different perspective.
- A grassed area for playing and picnics in dry weather.
- A paved area for wet weather: this should be wide enough for use of wheeled toys.
- Some means of shade.
- Some means of seating: informal log seats fixed into the ground are suitable and cheap.
- Winding tracks using different surfaces, e.g. crazy paving, brick patterns and cobbles.
- A small growing and digging area.
- A wild garden with buddleia bushes, long grass and rotting logs to attract insects.
- A sandpit with paved surroundings and a secure cover.

Use of space

- Visit a range of nursery environments and consider how space is used. Jot down impressions during your visit or take a photograph as an *aide-mémoire*. It is also helpful to visit a setting during a working session and again later without children.
- Consider what is possible. Draw a scale plan of your nursery and a separate list of the experiences you want to offer during a term. Identify the fixed activity areas and see where there is scope for flexibility in other areas.

Check that your room arrangement supports your principles

Consider how your room:

- Helps you to regard children as individuals; e.g. through providing for special needs – a punch-bag in a corner of the room is excellent therapy for some children.
- Helps toward continuity of learning; e.g. there should be some aspect of room arrangement that will be reproduced when the child moves to main school.
- Helps the child learn through his actions and through talk; e.g. provision of learning bays to accommodate small groups of children – these may be created with mobile furniture to give the illusion of privacy for the children but offering the adult the ability to oversee.
- Helps the child develop as an early mathematician; e.g. create enclosed spaces for play and display on different levels to encourage spatial awareness.
- Helps the child learn through a broad curriculum; e.g. low storage lockers with open shelves containing a range of media for children to select in making their representations.
- Helps the child have a balanced curriculum; e.g. arrange for unstructured materials for child-initiated as well as teacher-directed activity.
- Helps the child to become an agent in his own learning; e.g. arrange the room for children to have easy access to resources – the painting area should be near the sink to allow for washing hands, and a low washing-line will allow children to hang up their paintings. Provide a cork-tiled wall area at child height for children to display their work.
- Helps the child to learn through success; e.g. some stable activity areas with familiar materials will offer less confident children the opportunity to learn at their own pace.
- Helps children to be regarded as people; e.g. aim for a comfortable, warm, bright environment that reflects an inviting atmosphere.

Equipment

- Check what you already have. Look systematically at all the apparatus and equipment there is to support different areas of learning; e.g. small construction play – check provision for the most and least able children; throw out incomplete or broken equipment, which will frustrate rather than aid children's learning; enlist parental help to mend equipment where possible.

- Agree priorities for spending in the light of your budget. It is more sensible to opt for resourcing one learning area properly than to spread money thinly across a range of activity.
- Establish clear criteria for purchasing further equipment; e.g. safety, quality, durability, multi-purpose use, easy storage, opportunity to extend learning, supportive to teacher's intention whether prescriptive or open-ended.
- Gather information about what is available. Visit other nurseries to see equipment in use; observe children using it and talk to teachers about specific strengths and limitations; send for sample kits; ask commercial representatives to visit your nursery and demonstrate what is on the market; press for regular exhibitions of equipment to be held at local teachers' centres; ask for advice from local inspectors and advisers.
- Monitor the effects of your decisions. Having made your purchases, carefully monitor how children use the equipment for the first term, noting what difference it has made both to individual children and to the group as a whole.

Consumable stock

- Keep an open stock-cupboard. Staff should be jointly responsible for keeping it tidy and for leaving a note when stocks of particular materials are low.
- Regularly review the quality and suitability of consumable materials; e.g. is the sand suitable? Should the type of clay be changed?
- Make collections of natural and junk materials; e.g. store collections of pebbles, shells and waste materials throughout the year. For conservation and learning purposes, the nursery should where possible grow its own produce to collect seed-heads and berries.

ORGANIZING THE PROGRAMME

Routines and programme structures are affected not only by how children are accommodated but also by the ratio of adults, the size of the group and the length and timing of the session. Three- and four-year-olds can have very different experiences; they may be at home with their parents, with a childminder or attending a playgroup for one or two part-time sessions a week; they may attend a private or state nursery class or school, a nursery centre or day nursery, or they may be admitted to an infant, first or primary school. Programmes may be part-time, full-time or for an extended day; they may be accommodated with a full nursery-age group, as a separate group of four-year-olds or with older children of school age. Provision is even more varied when geographical location is considered. Some nursery provision may be within walking distance; or children may have to travel with their parents across an urban area, or take a circuitous route on the school bus from an outlying area to the village school, which will greatly affect the length of their day. In such diverse circumstances, it is impossible to give hard-and-fast guidance on programmes which will be helpful to all. The child's well-being is all-important, and once again curriculum principles and theories of child development must determine the pace and pattern of the day.

Recent studies nevertheless give pointers to programme planning, and this guidance can be interpreted and followed in different settings. There is a danger, though, as Lesley Webb warned: 'A practice is not adequately described or justified by its naming, and a common label by no means indicates common practice.' She suggests that some of the terms used to describe a programme can be interpreted in many ways:

> In one nursery school 'reception' may involve a brisk whirling of children from parents and into vigorous activity within ten minutes of the beginning of the school day; in another the process may spread over an hour of staggered entry, with leisurely chat, mothers helping teachers, and a generally unhurried 'run in' to activities.[10]

Until the early 1970s the two extreme approaches to nursery programmes were centred upon either (1) rich, stimulating environments for children to use freely as they wish, within the boundaries of safety, or (2) structured, compensatory programmes heavily based on drills and behaviour modification, as followed in the United States by Bereiter and Engelmann.[11] Whilst the first was based very firmly on the therapeutic value of play and devalued the place of intellectual development, the latter emphasized the need for isolated skills to be taught to young children in a highly directive way, to 'top them up' before entering mainstream school.

This polarized view of appropriate programmes was reinforced by Marion Blank's suggestion that there should exist two types of 'preschools'. She describes the first as the 'shared rearing' pre-school programme, which aims 'to provide a secure, benign environment that is compatible with the interests and predispositions of the children'. The second type is the 'academic pre-school', which focuses on the child with learning needs; there the intention is 'to structure the information, material and language in extremely precise ways . . . to alter the child's level of functioning in the entire academic sphere'.[12] It is only fair to say, however, that Blank's suggestions for fostering this approach are based on developing communication techniques rather than on drills and lessons. A third approach that has already been mentioned in this book is the High Scope programme, devised by David Weikart. Cognitive development is again stressed, but the programme supports the notion that children learn through first-hand experiences and offers teachers a clear framework to allow child-centred and adult-initiated activity.

The teacher's task is to aim for the most valuable programme for her children. Let us now see how these programmes stand in relation to current research. The Oxford Pre-School Research Project gives little support to the didactic programmes which emphasize role learning and a heavy reliance on teaching materials. Sylva's work values the child-centred nursery but emphasizes that simply having solid blocks of time for child-selected activity is not enough:

> The British nursery school and playgroup is justly famous for the amount of free choice it offers children. Our data do not support a major revolution in this policy – only a shift towards 'punctuating' the free regime with required educational tasks. When this is done the free play becomes more than a time for letting off steam; it's a period for consolidation and expansion.[13]

Teachers of young children often emphasize the importance of routine, to ensure security and build the child's confidence. But Lesley Webb rightly warns us of routines that are unthinkingly applied:

> There is a higher proportion of time spent in some nursery schools on non-educative pursuits apart from socialization . . . examples recently observed are: compulsory listening to stories (except that children do not actually listen when made to sit down and look as if they are); children desultorily looking at rubbishy picture-books; constant interruptions of absorbed play, in order to get children to drink milk, change shoes, go outside, wash hands . . . all could be corrected or eliminated at the cost of more thought about the intentions of nursery education.[14]

Sylva distinguishes between the regularity of tasks and the structure in the task. She concludes that, where specially planned educational tasks are offered within the framework of a flexible routine, this enhances learning; the daily repetition of activities and schedules, by contrast, may have little effect.

Sylva's comparative study of nurseries in Miami and Oxfordshire offers further support for a modified traditional nursery programme. She suggests that in Oxfordshire, where the children were able to start and end activities at will, there was often a strong link between the length of concentration and the complexity of the task. This did not happen in Miami, where the emphasis was on long sessions of teacher-directed activity that was often of a low level of challenge.[15]

Sylva's study usefully focused on intellectual development in young children. However, when investigating the effects of the three types of programme outlined earlier in this section, Weikart's findings suggest that there may be a link between the programme style and the child's future social and emotional achievements. This long-term study revealed that a group of fifteen-year-olds who had previously followed a directive behaviourist nursery programme had been involved in many more incidents of delinquency, vandalism and drug abuse than matched groups who had followed traditional and High Scope programmes in the nursery.[16] These findings must be treated with caution, since only sixty-eight children altogether were studied. But there is still an implication that social responsibility is linked with a child-initiated style of early education. With heavy teacher direction the child has little opportunity to make choices or to develop a self-directed approach to life.

This latest indicator is particularly helpful in focusing attention on the children as people. Weikart himself stresses that 'We've got to stop looking at academic variables as the only criteria for effective behaviour.'

In some nurseries there is discretion as to whether children are offered a part-time or full-time placement. Such decisions are often made solely on the basis of social need and family circumstance, but there is also a need to consider the relative effectiveness of the different timing and length of sessions. Unfortunately there is a lack of British research in this area, and US studies have been contradictory in their findings,[17] or have found no significant difference.[18]

One useful piece of research compared the effects of half-day and alternative-day provision on academic achievement, classroom social behaviour and children's attendance.[19] Although no difference was found in the academic achievements of the two groups, the children who had attended for alternate full days scored higher on factors of originality and independent learning; these factors included developing materials in the classroom, using materials in new ways, the urge to explore and converse more, powers of conversation and the ability to organize and collect materials for work. It seems likely that, given at one stretch a longer period of time to become familiar with the environment, children have a greater chance of achieving in these areas.

Teachers' own opinions of alternate full-day attendance tended to be negative. They considered that, although there was no difference in the number of hours spent in the nursery, the lack of daily contact meant a loss of continuity for alternate-day children and a lack of concentration during the afternoon sessions of a full day.

Teachers need to look closely at the type of programme that can be planned for part-time and full-time children and whether it is possible or desirable to be flexible with placements. Administratively there may be problems in allowing one child to attend for one or two part-time sessions weekly while another is admitted on a full-time basis. From the child's point of view, however, beginning with part-time attendance may make for an easier transition to the nursery.

In most areas the ratio of professionals employed in a nursery will be fixed. Unless there is enhanced staffing for special circumstances, in educational establishments it is likely that one adult will be employed for every ten children in a nursery school and for every fifteen children in a class. In areas where four-year-olds are admitted into school, staffing levels may be as low as one to thirty children. Playgroup staff ratios, on the other hand, are much higher – one argument being the need for more adults in buildings which are not purpose built and where many of the helpers are untrained.

Serious consideration must be given to what can be achieved with large groups of children, given a poor staffing ratio. Sylva argues strongly for small units. She found a direct link between the size of playgroup or nursery, the number of adults employed and the intellectual level of children's play. She suggests that a good staff–child ratio is one to ten or under, and an excellent ratio one to seven and under.[20] One of the major constraints found in the Miami nurseries was the low staffing levels, which varied from one adult to anything between ten and twenty-five children.

Woods points out the dangers of one teacher coping with a large group of children:

> The answer to the problem of scarce human resources cannot rest in an overly organized curriculum based on children acting in concert and in groups. Children are quite limited in their ability to comprehend or show interest in extended thought or talk about experiences removed from their own activities or home life. We should not be bullied by political proclamations about the proper level or provision of teacher resources for the young child. Our yardstick should not be some politically or economically expedient half-truth based on a convenient theory but one based in actual observations of the quality, depth and extent of contacts between individual children and responsive adults in different situations.[21]

The British Association for Early Childhood Education and the Pre-School Playgroup Association are both concerned with the educational programmes being offered to four-year-olds in many local authority areas. In a joint statement they describe some of the needs of this age group:

> Most four-year-old children are not ready to be confined to crowded classrooms without scope for physical and imaginative play. They are still mastering basic physical skills for which they need opportunities not generally found in the primary classroom. They are happier with a group of their peers and younger children than with those older than themselves. They need plenty of opportunities to ask questions and talk with adults informally. They are constantly experimenting and look to adults for approval and attention at frequent intervals. For these reasons the higher ratio of adults to children available at home, with a childminder or in playgroups and nursery classes is more appropriate at this stage.[22]

The use of properly briefed volunteers is one answer to offer children time and attention. Where there are strong objections to this, the onus is on teachers to refuse to admit children when they know that they are unable to offer them a programme of quality.

Suggested action

Plan your programme to allow time for work with children and parents

- Prepare your physical environment and materials for activities well before the beginning of the session. In this way you are free to greet children and parents on arrival.
- Plan for a leisured start and end to the day; e.g. staggered entry and collection of children are helpful – these are best managed if children start and end the day with small-group activity.
- Plan a programme that is manageable; e.g. have a range of self-maintaining activities for children, putting priority on well-resourced construction and role-play. You should not be tied to a group of children because of an excessively teacher-directed activity.
- Plan for children to care for their own environment; e.g. teach children where to find materials and show clear expectations about how they should be returned; allow plenty of time for clearing away at the end of a session and spend time showing children how to do this rather than doing it yourself.

Make your daily routines support the well-being and learning of the child

- Avoid wasting time; e.g. allow for children's involvement in activity immediately they enter the nursery – formal register-taking is inappropriate, although a head count of children should take place at an early stage in the session.
- Plan large-group activities when children are most receptive; a group story or jingle time is not necessarily best received at the end of the day.
- Avoid unnecessary interruptions during the session; the emphasis should be on blocks of time for child-initiated activity.
- Plan some predictable routines; children will quickly learn that at some stage during the session there is a change of activity, a narrowing of curriculum choice, or that lunchtime is preceded by washing hands and laying the table.

Plan a nursery programme for four-year-olds admitted to an infant school

- Develop a sensitive admissions policy. This should mean a staggered entry of children over a period of time, initially on a part-time basis. Admissions in October allow the teacher to visit every home in September and to build on this knowledge of children's past experience.
- Be flexible about the pattern of attendance. Four-year-old children may find school attendance very tiring initially, particularly if it is full-time.
- You should be particularly sympathetic to irregular attendance if the child is travelling from a rural area to attend school for a full day.
- Ensure that parents of four-year-olds are aware of their child's developmental needs; enlist their support for an integrated day with a large measure of child-initiated activity.
- If possible arrange for a separate entrance to school, with the opportunity for parents to accompany their children into the classroom.
- Plan for four-year-olds to have a separate playtime from the main school and a shortened lunch break, with opportunities for children to be inside or outside.
- Avoid four-year-olds being involved with large assemblies, particularly with a full primary age group. Plan for a separate gathering or one which is shared with another infant class.

ORGANIZING TEACHING AND LEARNING

The teacher's role in facilitating children's learning has been subject to a range of interpretation. In past years a polarized view developed reflecting the two types of programme outlined previously. On the one hand, there was a passive style, with the teacher providing the rich environment but viewing any direct involvement with children as intrusive rather than helpful to learning; the opposite style was highly directive, with the teacher setting up situations, instructing children and requiring a response. In simplistic terms, the one can be seen to be an abrogation of responsibility for promoting learning, while the other diminishes the child's elective and active role as learner.

Today the teacher is seen as a vital resource in promoting learning and development. This must mean a close look at how teachers manage their time and how they work with children. A nursery environment is undoubtedly a complex and busy one. To bring together a group of children who are egocentric with short concentration spans and a great deal of energy is no easy matter, and to enable them to engage in a variety of first-hand experiences requires the teacher to have high organizational skills. The danger of this is that the organization can become an end in itself. In trying to ensure that the nursery programme does not disintegrate, the teacher can spend her time overseeing the activities, interacting superficially and briefly with children and neglecting her key role of helping children to develop and understand.

In the playgroups he visited, Woods found that where the adults took on a heavy management role they were approached by children about management matters. The adults who played and talked with the children were more often approached about personal interactions. Thus, he suggests, 'the adult is pulled deeper and deeper into managerial action by the children themselves'.[23]

The number of adults available to children will affect the style of organization. The teacher's role in organizing these other adults is discussed in Chapter 6; however, there is the assumption that as a 'leader' of any such team the teacher will take on the overseeing role in the nursery, deploying nursery assistants and parents to work in more depth with small groups and individuals. If this is a predominant way of working it will mean that the teacher's skills are not properly employed in teaching.

We have stressed the need for children to learn to be self-sufficient. This is both in their own interest and also to ensure that the teacher does not have to try to cope with all their learning needs at the same time. In a well-organized nursery some children can be profitably involved in activity without the presence of an adult. Having managed to gain time for herself, then, we are concerned with what the teacher does with this time – how she works to facilitate learning.

Young children's learning is promoted by the teacher's role as observer, planner, tutor, conversationalist, questioner, instructor and model. Let us consider each of these roles briefly. (The teacher is also an assessor and evaluator, and these aspects of her work are included in Chapter 6.)

Teacher as observer

Observation is a skill introduced to teachers in training. We would expect the nursery teacher to have internalized this skill and carried it into the classroom as the very pivot for practice. Lesley Webb describes what it involves:

> The seeing eye can be trained, as can most senses, and the more we train ourselves to observe the more we see even when we are not actually making a child-study. Noticing what they really do, how, when and in what order, becomes a habit with the good teacher. Like all habits it can be encouraged by letting the novice practise it frequently. Once established, the ability to look without prejudice, to note detail, to assess a child's pace, needs and strengths, makes for realistic goal-setting and consequent success and satisfaction for the child and teacher alike.[24]

Observation is time-consuming, but the experienced teacher will learn how to fit it into her daily routine and also to identify who she needs to observe. Observation is the basis for developing the learning of all children, but more information is required about some individuals than about others.

Although teachers must learn to appear casual and unobtrusive when observing and recording, it is important that the process is structured. The Schools Council project on record-keeping in primary schools offers advice to teachers wanting to improve their observation of children:

1. Determine in advance what to observe but be alert for unusual behaviour.
2. Observe and record enough of the situation to make the behaviour meaningful.
3. Make a record of the incident as soon after the observation as possible.
4. Limit each anecdote to a brief description of a single incident.
5. Keep the factual description of the incident and your interpretation of it separate. Use only non-judgemental words in the description.
6. Record both negative and positive behavioural incidents.
7. Collect a number of anecdotes on a pupil before drawing inferences concerning typical behaviour.[25]

Observations of children must also go hand in hand with a knowledge of child development. This knowledge can help teachers to observe aspects of behaviour which might not otherwise have been noticed; it will help make observations more objective, and will offer a theoretical framework to help interpret and explain the behaviour observed.

Teacher as planner

The teacher's planning will capitalize on what she has observed in the nursery. Having planned the environment and taken into account what assistance she has, she can plan where to spend her time. She may recognize that one particular play area is not very popular, and decide that her own involvement and interaction may encourage children to use it more. The teacher should also plan with whom she will spend time. Katz draws attention to the 'recursive cycle':

> the fact that having a given characteristic or behaviour such as high verbal ability stimulates responses from others which lead to strengthening it. Thus the more verbally able a child, the more verbal input he or she receives from adults and the more verbally able the child becomes. . . . Thus a planned programme of positive discrimination is necessary to support learning and development in less able children.[26]

The teacher also has an important role in planning for children to interact with one another. Rubin focuses on the varying social skills that children bring into school, and Scarlett looks at the children who lack many of these skills and become social isolates. The two studies suggest that the adult can help children to develop friendship skills by engineering pairs of children to be together and providing structured play in which relatively isolated children can interact more with other children. However, promoting this aspect of development is a sensitive area; Rubin warns that adults should be aware of the fine line that exists between help and interference. 'Rather than "pushing" social skills indiscriminately, adults should respect the real differences between children that motivate some to establish friendly relationships with many others, some to concentrate on one or two close friendships and some to spend a good deal of time by themselves.'[27]

We previously examined how children can help one another through interaction and talk (see page 40). Dewhirst suggests that in planning these opportunities the teacher's own management style is important. She found that the more instructional the approach, the less likely children were to talk together: 'children had time to explore and develop these contexts [for talk] with maximum teacher support and involvement in terms of making the settings attractive and available, but with the minimum of interruption and overt direction'.[28]

Teacher as tutor

In his study of socially isolated children Scarlett found that they were less likely to become involved in imaginative role-play.[29] It may be that these children need active help in learning to play symbolically. Smilansky and Freyburg found that children who received such assistance made noticeable gains in their play. Smilansky called this process 'pump priming'. If the child does not react in an imaginative setting, she suggests that the teacher plays and reacts as if the child were role-playing.[30] She might say, 'Good morning, Mrs Brown. Has your husband gone to work today? I am going shopping. Do you want me to buy you anything from the shops? Oh, here is Mrs Green, who is coming to have a cup of coffee with you.'

Freyburg played with a small group of children using pipe-cleaner dolls and other improvised materials. She worked with the children to act out prepared stories. When these children were compared with a control group they were found to have improved their powers of imagination and concentration.[31]

The teacher's role as a play tutor may be necessary as a bridge to enable some children to take part in active role-play with their peers. As the child grows in confidence and becomes more responsive, the teacher can take a less obtrusive role but should withdraw only when her target child is established in a group.

Teacher as conversationalist

The teacher's role as play tutor is specific to certain children. Her role in promoting talk, however, although easier with some individuals than with others, is important for all. Her aim should be to enable all children to share their feelings, thoughts, ideas and attitudes with her. To achieve this, a particular style of working is required.

Woods explores how adults can help children converse with them freely and openly. His transcripts of many adult–child conversations reveal that the adult who offers her own personal views, ideas and observations tends to receive many of the child's views; there is a genuine sharing of experience. Conversely, the adult who controls the conversation and who asks questions persistently may receive answers but seldom elaborations or opinions. The conversation thus becomes dominated by the adult:

> The apparent maturity and competence of the pre-school child in conversation, then, is not only dependent upon his language ability or home background, but also upon the framework that the adult sets for him in dialogue. The more she is inclined or driven to ask questions and exercise control to keep him going, the less likely she is to be successful. By leaving the child time to think, and periodically taking the pressure off to reveal something of her thoughts, she is most likely to see him at his linguistically most active.[32]

Both Woods and Sylva argue that the managerial nature of the work of a nursery teacher means that, during the day, talk tends to comprise brief, trivial comments relating to the control of children and the organization of activities. It is all too easy for the teacher to spend her day seeing that the water is not spilt, sand not thrown, helping children to put on aprons, do up coats and wash their hands, without having had time to engage in sustained talk with an individual or group of children. The point is that time must be made to promote children's conversation.

Sylva stresses the need for the 'subtle tutorial' to take place between adult and child or small group. She sees this in the context of an activity with a clear goal structure involving the adult encouraging the child towards elaboration of this task. Thus, with large construction apparatus the teacher may admire the building of a castle but continue to ask about the location of the entrance, how the castle is made secure and how it is defended. According to Sylva, the adult enters the child's construction task with related conversation, which is what another child cannot do.[33]

Tizard and Hughes suggest that many of the valuable opportunities young children have for conversing occur at home during involvement with routine chores.[34] This too has implications for the way the teacher uses her time; nursery routines can be productive occasions for dialogue.

Teacher as questioner

Woods warns of the danger of imposing too many questions on children, yet teachers are aware of the need to ask questions as a way of checking children's understanding. Marion Blank, for instance, suggests that one valuable area of discussion can centre on materials which undergo changes in state. Questions may centre on the process (considering cakes before and after cooking and seeing what has changed), on memory (children remembering what they could do with sand before they added water to it) and on cause and effect (what has to happen to turn an ice cube back into water?).[35]

However, questioning should not be overrated as a process. Hughes and Grieve suggest that we should not assume that children will reveal their lack of knowledge or understanding through questioning. Their study presented five-year-olds with questions intended to be unanswerable (e.g. 'Is milk heavier than water?' 'Is red bigger than yellow?'). They invariably received some answer, and, when asked why, the children responded by adding their own meaning to the question (e.g. milk was found to be heavier than water because it came out of a bottle and water came out of a tap).[36] This study supports another, which indicates that young children will respond to questions when the meaning to them may be quite obscure.[37]

All conversation tends to include questions. But these should perhaps stem from the adult's interest in eliciting the child's viewpoint, rather than be a testing technique.

Teacher as instructor

The teacher's role as instructor is not intended in any formal, restricted sense but simply to highlight that the teacher should provide help, offer information and teach certain skills. Woods suggests that, 'where adults do not supply such a framework for a child in a difficult task, he may well become demoralized, losing interest in the activity and confidence in his own ability'.[38] Vygotsky claimed that instruction and imitation are both powerful tools in the child's development. He suggested that what the child can do in co-operation today he can do alone tomorrow.[39]

Teacher as model

We have considered the importance of the teacher as the model through which the young child bases his view of the world (see Chapter 2). This modelling influences the child's social abilities and strengthens his intellectual skills. Bruner, supporting the place of intuitive thinking in learning, comments: 'it seems unlikely that a student would develop or have confidence in his intuitive methods of thinking if he never saw them used effectively by his elders'.[40]

Katz suggests that offering a model will aid a child's communication skills:

> This approach has been illustrated in a situation in which one child complains to the teacher that another will not let her have a turn with the tricycle. In such a case the teacher can say to the complaining child something like, 'It might help to say to (the other child) I've been waiting a long time and I really want a turn', adding, 'And if that doesn't work, come back and we'll think of something else to try.' The teacher models a tone of moderate but firm assertiveness the child can imitate.

Katz also argues that young children need an adult model of articulateness and the opportunity to share in adult thinking: 'Teachers might be encouraged to speak to children as though they are real people, albeit with limited experiences and vocabularies; they are not pets or dolls and should be spoken to seriously.'[41]

Suggested action

Teacher as observer

Aim to build observation into your programme on a regular basis, particularly using times when you have additional adult help from parents or students.

- Observe children's behaviour:
  - Time-sample a child's total behaviour during the course of a week to gain a general picture of how he spends his time, and with whom. Aim to note and record the behaviour for two minutes every half-hour.
  - Time-sample specific behaviour. Using the same technique, record only predetermined behaviour such as aggression, temper tantrums or solitary play. The evidence gained may prevent a child being labelled due to the assumption that the behaviour occurs more than it does.
  - Observe over a period of time. Aim to tackle at least one longitudinal study a year, observing a child weekly from September to July, to check his rate of progress in development; e.g. powers of concentration, development of fine motor skills and use of language.
- Observe activity. Study activity areas in the nursery to note who uses them, when they are most used and how the equipment is used. This information will help you make decisions about siting and about the form of the provision and how it might be better used.
- Record information using different formats:
  - Keep duplicated copies of a nursery plan, indicating the location of various activities. Use this plan for charting and recording the child's movements during the course of the session (Figure 2).

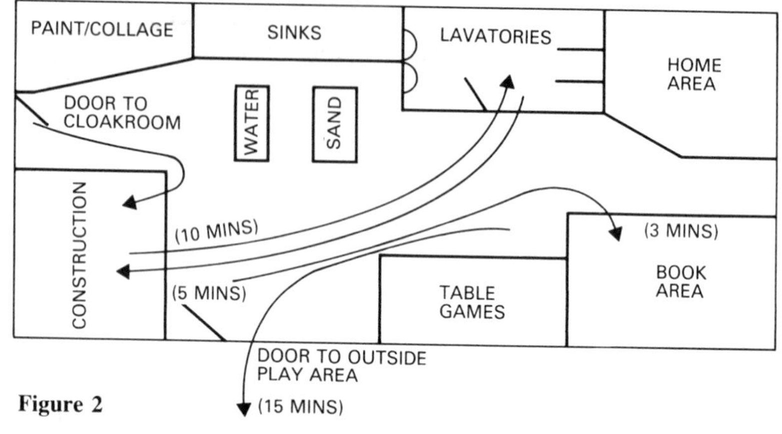

Figure 2

– Record children's small-group interactions as a simple sociogram. Draw a line every time a child initiates talk, with the arrow pointing to the child he addresses. This is a time-consuming and demanding task but is occasionally worthwhile, especially in providing a picture of isolates and children who dominate conversations (Figure 3).

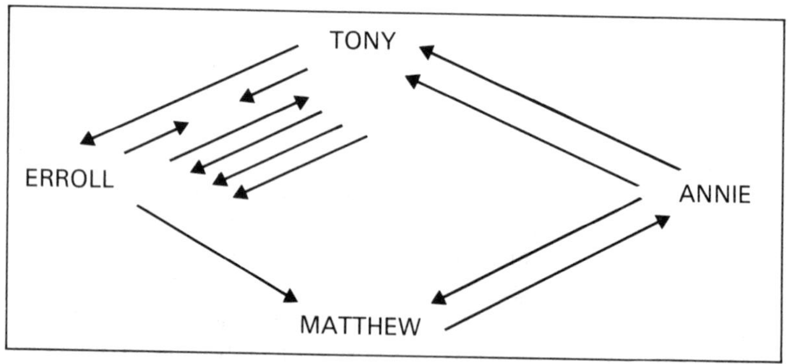

Figure 3

Teacher as planner

Teacher presence at an activity automatically stimulates children's interest. During a term you should aim to spend time at each activity to see the range of play, how the provision is used and how it supports learning.

- Plan to work in depth with children; ensure that your nursery assistant keeps an overseeing eye on the nursery as a whole while you work with a target group of children.
- Plan time with new children; arrange to be available to new children and make it a priority to spend part of every session with them until they have settled.
- Plan time to work with children who do not respond easily; make sure that these children are regularly involved with you as individuals in shopping trips or in domestic routines such as cleaning the hamster's cage.
- Plan to spend time with the most able children; initiate challenging problems involving small-scale constructions – building an obstacle course, creating sound patterns and recording them on cassettes, reading with real books.
- Plan individual programmes for children; if a child is failing in a task, plan a variety of tasks in which he is introduced to sub-skills – e.g. if unable to use scissors, tearing paper; small constructional work and finger-rhymes designed to strengthen small muscles (see Appendix II).

Teacher as conversationalist

- Take time to listen to children; make their interests your starting-point.
- Share your own personal experiences with children. They will respond warmly to news about your own children or your purchase of a new dress or new puppy or looking at your holiday photographs (let them bring some of theirs).
- Share your views with children as a way of eliciting theirs; e.g. 'I thought that our ride on the bus this morning was a bit bumpy. Did you, Joe?'
- Include and involve other children; e.g. 'Well, Ros, I don't know what colour paint to use. Ask Neil what he thinks.'

Teacher as questioner

- Avoid questions to which it is obvious you already have the answer.
- Try to question children when you are both involved in a shared activity. This should result in a more natural discourse and a sharing of views rather than interrogation.
- Be sensitive to the time that different children need in giving a response; this will mean waiting to allow some children time to

gather their thoughts, but not so long that the silence means pressure which will inhibit their answers.

Teacher as instructor

- Be aware of when a child requires help. Always respond to his request for help, even if the assistance you give is in the form of suggestions and advice rather than taking on the task yourself.
- The younger the child the more personal and active must be the instruction. Three- and four-year-olds are more likely to respond to individual instruction with the adult demonstrating and then being prepared to assist; e.g. showing the child how to do up his coat by standing behind him and guiding his movements.

Teacher as model

- Offer the child a model of questioning; e.g. 'If you want to know how much water you need to mix the paint, why don't you ask James? Say "How much water did you need when you mixed the paint yesterday, James?"'
- Work alongside the child at your own level, offering a model of interest and concentration rather than showing a standard of work to be achieved; e.g. join children when they are drawing from observation or creating patterns.
- Offer a model of thinking for children; e.g. 'I wanted to buy some shoes the same colour as my new dress. I wanted exactly the same colour, but it was too cold to wear my dress when I went to the shop. So I wrapped the dress up in a parcel and took it with me. I shoed the shop lady and she found me shoes that are exactly right. Look – can you see?'

REFERENCES

1 J. Dewey. *The School and Society*, University of Chicago Press, Chicago, 1915.
2 Lady Allen of Hurtwood, *Planning for Play*, Thames and Hudson, London, 1968.
3 S. Neill, 'Open plan or divided space in pre-school?', *Education 3–13*, Vol. 10, Autumn 1982, p. 46.
4 K. Sylva, C. Roy and M. Painter, *Child Watching at Playgroup and Nursery School*, Grant McIntyre, London, 1980. P. K. Smith and K. J. Connolly. *The Ecology of Pre School Behaviour*, Cambridge University Press, 1981.
5 K. Bathurst, 'The need for national nurseries', *Nineteenth Century*, May 1905, pp. 818–27.

6 M. Hohmann, B. Banet and D. Weikart, *Young Children in Action*, High Scope Press, Ypsilanti, Mich., 1979.
7 J. S. Bruner, *Child Care: Science, Art and Technology*, The Gilchrist Lecture, 1978.
8 M. A. Pulaski, 'Toys and imaginative play', in J. L. Singer (ed.), *The Child's World of Make Believe*, Academic Press, London, 1973.
9 Sylva, Roy and Painter, op. cit. (note 4).
10 L. Webb, *Purpose and Practice of Nursery Education*, Blackwell, Oxford, 1974.
11 C. Bereiter and S. Englemann, *Teaching Disadvantaged Children in the Pre-school*, Prentice-Hall, Englewood Cliffs, NJ, 1966.
12 M. Blank, 'Pre-school and/or education: a comment', in M. Roberts and J. Tamburrini (eds.), *Child Development 0–5*, Holmes McDougall, Edinburgh, 1981.
13 Sylva, Roy and Painter, op. cit. (note 4).
14 Webb, op. cit. (note 10).
15 Sylva, Roy and Painter, op. cit. (note 4).
16 D. Weikart, reported in *Times Educational Supplement*, May 25, 1986, p. 13.
17 D. J. Gornovich, R. C. Volker and R. Landry, *A School District Looks at an Alternative to Half Day, Every Day Kindergarten Programs*, Grand Rapids (Mich.) Independent School District; ERIC Document Reproduction Service, No. ED 107 347, 1974. F. L. Pigge, *A Two-Year Comparative Study of the Possible Effects of Alternate Day, Full Day, and Daily Half Day Organizational Patterns*, Bowling Green (Ohio) State University, 1979.
18 Minnesota State Department of Education, *Kindergarten Evaluation Study: Full Day Alternate Programs*, St. Paul, Minn.; ERIC Document Reproduction Service, No. ED 070 529, 1972. A. J. Mouw, *The Description and Evaluation of the Alternate Day-Full Day Kindergarten Program*, Madison, Wisconsin, Public Schools; ERIC Document Reproduction Service, No. ED 129, 435, 1976.
19 D. F. Gullo and D. H. Clements, 'The effects of kindergarten schedule on achievement, classroom behavior and attendance', *Journal of Educational Research*, Vol. 78, No. 1, pp. 51–6.
20 Sylva, Roy and Painter, op. cit. (note 4).
21 D. Woods, L. McMahan and Y. Cranstoun, *Working with Under-Fives*, Grant McIntyre, London, 1980.
22 Pre-School Playgroups Association and British Association for Early Childhood Education, *Four Years Old but Not Yet Five*, London, 1985.
23 Woods, McMahan and Cranstoun, op. cit. (note 21).
24 L. Webb, *Making a Start on a Child Study*, Blackwell, Oxford, 1975.
25 P. Shields, G. Weiner and E. Wilson, *Record-Keeping in Primary Schools*, Schools Council/Macmillan, London, 1981.
26. L. G. Katz, 'Fostering communicative competence in young children', in M. M. Clark (ed.), *Helping Communication in Early Education*, Educational Review Occasional Publications No. 11, 1985.
27 Z. Rubin, 'The skills of friendship', in M. Donaldson (ed.), *Early Childhood Development and Education*, Blackwell, Oxford, 1983.
28 E. Dewhirst, 'Settings as contexts for dialogue: guidelines for practice in the management and organization of communication between children', in M. M. Clark (ed.), op. cit. (note 26).

29 W. G. Scarlett, 'Social isolation from age mates among nursery school children', in M. Donaldson (ed.), op. cit. (note 27).
30 S. Smilansky, *The Effects of Sociodramatic Play on Disadvantaged Children*, Wiley, Chichester, 1968.
31 J. T. Freyburg, 'Increasing the imaginative play of urban disadvantaged kindergarten children through systematic training', in J. L Singer (ed.), op. cit. (note 8).
32 Woods, McMahan and Cranstoun, op. cit. (note 21).
33 Sylva, Roy and Painter, op. cit. (note 4).
34 B. Tizard and M. Hughes, *Young Children Learning*, Fontana, London, 1984.
35 M. Blank, 'Classroom discourse: the neglected topic of the topic', in M. M. Clark (ed.), op. cit. (note 26).
36 M. Hughes and R. Grieve, 'On asking children bizzare questions', in M. Donaldson (ed.), op. cit. (note 27).
37 R. N. Campbell and T. Bowe, 'Functional/asymmetry in early language understanding', in G. Drachman (ed.), *Salzburger Beitrage für Linguistik* Vol. 3, Gunter Narr, Tubingen, 1977.
38 Woods, McMahan and Cranstoun, op. cit. (note 21).
39 L. S. Vygotsky, 'School instruction and mental development' (1962), in M. Donaldson (ed.), op. cit. (note 27).
40 Bruner, op. cit. (note 7).
41 Katz, op. cit. (note 26).

5

HOW IS IT SUCCEEDING?

The best practitioners have always been concerned about what and how learning is transmitted to children. However, all schools in all phases of education are now aware of the need to look very carefully and to satisfy themselves that they are being effective. This need for greater scrutiny stems from increased demands from central and local government and from parents for schools to be more accountable. Central government's growing interest in curriculum relating to the five-to-sixteen age range is demonstrated by the range of DES and HMI documents published since the late 1970s and recent government White Papers.

In *Teaching Quality* there is a declared intention 'to make the best use of available resources to maintain and improve standards in education'.[1] In *Better Schools* the argument is that teachers need to know how they perform with children, so that they may be 'helped to respond to changing demands and to realize their professional potential'.[2] Circulars 6/81 and 8/83 required local education authorities to declare their intentions for ensuring that every boy and girl has a curriculum suited to his or her abilities, age and aptitudes.[3] This resulted in local authority curriculum policy statements which in many cases made explicit the educational principles and practices that schools were expected to promote.

The right of parents to become more informed and involved in their child's education is stressed in *Better Schools*. This right is also reflected in the increased representation of parents on governing bodies made possible through the 1980 Education Act. Parents are now also increasingly aware of their rights in choosing a school and are able to read any HMI reports on a school, since these are openly published.

The nursery teacher must be as concerned with this issue of accountability as other teachers, because nursery education is still funded by public money. Non-statutory provision is always vulnerable in times of economic restraint, and even if nursery provision is not abandoned it may be 'modified'. Undesirable thrifty measures may be introduced which in effect offer three- and four-year-olds a travesty of the education they need.

Properly resourced nurseries, with space, good-quality equipment and the right number of well-trained adults, cost money. Where this exists the onus is on the teacher to prove the effectiveness of such provision. Where less is offered, there is still a need for a careful scrutiny of results for the teacher to be clear about what she can achieve and where she is forced to compromise due to lack of resources.

Some measures by central and local government have emphasized its own role in requiring accountability. The development of the Assessment of Performance Unit to monitor children's attainments at different stages,[4] the compulsory screening of all children by local authorities, and whole-school inspections are just some of the external initiatives that have been introduced. Nursery children are not themselves involved in any testing procedures, but nurseries are open to inspections by HMI and local authority officers.

'Accountability' is no longer a new term. The teacher is contractually accountable to those who pay her salary and morally and professionally accountable to her clients – the parents and children. Teachers need to be told how they are performing, but more than this is required if they are to respond effectively to changing demands or to improve their performance. While external appraisal and prescriptive documents can help to make teachers aware of their strengths and weaknesses, there is no guarantee that this knowledge will be accepted and acted upon. In some circumstances it can have adverse effect, causing anxiety and feelings of inadequacy if 'recipes for improvement' are not forthcoming. Conversely, if the teacher can be helped to take responsibility for examining her practice and the nursery service offered she will be strengthened professionally.

In this chapter we consider steps that nursery teachers can take to develop self-evaluation. They need to decide which aspects of their work merit closer attention or review, and this will involve gathering specific information through a monitoring process. Where progress can be measured, assessments should be made and recorded, and this information will be useful in evaluating whatever aspect of the nursery is being considered.

REVIEW AND MONITORING

HMI describe 'review' as 'a retrospective activity [which] implies the collection and examination of evidence and information'.[5] Reviews may be tackled as a team or by individual teachers. The review process can vary from informal staff discussion about some aspect of school life to a highly structured questionnaire which is offered to the staff to complete to decide which aspects of work merit closer attention. The initial stages in the 'GRIDS' programme are an example of the latter approach and are very suitable for a staff new to monitoring and review.[6] HMI comment: 'For schools that were used to evaluation, the information-gathering stage was less formal and detailed.'[7]

'Monitoring' is the term given to information gathering. In *The Practical Curriculum* monitoring is likened to 'taking an invalid's temperature or checking tyre pressure and oil levels, a thing to be done carefully, from time to time, as a prelude to assessment and review'.[8] Monitoring is something that is built into most teachers' practice, because it involves keeping in touch with the effects of teaching and learning. The process may extend outside the classroom to include parental and community links, continuity and liaison, staff development and all other aspects that impinge on the life of the school. Any systematic approach to monitoring needs to regard each of these strands in turn and to consider the best means of gathering the information required. It may need to take into account information from children, colleagues, parents and governors, as well as one's own behaviour and responses.

Monitoring thus requires skills which can be learnt but which should not be underemphasized. Some of the monitoring skills required by teachers engaged in self-evaluation are described in the Open University material *Curriculum in Action*:

> Ability to carry out observations including: an ability to recognize the selective nature of observations, the implications of selecting a sample of pupils, the implications of using a particular recording technique, the implications of selecting a focus for observation. An ability to categorize data from observations. An ability to recognize inferences made while observing, recording and categorizing information.[9]

Time and planning are needed to identify the area to be monitored. Where observations are made, they need to be structured; an *aide-mémoire* can be helpful. Many of the suggestions for action in this book have focused on issues for teachers to monitor. However, the complexity of classroom life means that self-monitoring can be a difficult and demanding task for the individual teacher. Information gathered from cassette and video recordings can be helpful, as can having an independent observer to gather information for the teacher. This latter approach was explored in a small-scale research project, Teachers in Partnership.[10] There the aims were explicit: to look at the ways in which teachers could learn from one another. The project monitored pairs of teachers, who alternated roles of 'observer' and 'teacher' and in turn gathered information for each other on issues they designated as causing concern.

The classroom observer needs to be seen by the teacher as a resource rather than a threat. The emphasis must be on the teacher being presented with objective evidence, which she will then use in making her own judgements. The team approach established in a nursery should provide a good foundation for this way of working. Nursery staff are used to working in the presence of other adults, and a nursery teacher and nursery assistant could develop 'partnership observation' as a regular aspect of their work, particularly during times when students are in the nursery.

In common with all schools, nurseries benefit from gaining information about themselves from lay people. HMI suggest that

> Greater recognition could also be given to the function of groups external to the school in the process of evaluation. Parents, governors, employers and the wider community have expectations of schools and of individual pupils. These need to be clearly articulated, and schools might do more to seek and consider these views.[11]

Suggested action

Review

- Using a 'GRIDS' approach, devise your own headings to consider with colleagues (one model is suggested in Appendix III).
- Give each member of staff in turn the responsibility of deciding on an aspect for whole-staff review in the nursery.

Monitoring

- Monitor content: consider the range of stories offered to children in one term; consider the range of imaginative play situations presented.
- Monitor routines:
  - Observe how children enter the nursery at the beginning of a session and what activities they seek.
  - Observe different behaviour of children when they are greeted

at the door and when the adults receive them at different activity areas.
  - Monitor the effect of changing a nursery routine; observe how children behave in a traditional whole-group set break time and then in a self-service snack break time.

- Monitor use of time:

  - Observe the number of choices that children are offered during a nursery session.
  - Use a student or teaching colleague to monitor how a nursery headteacher uses her time during the course of a day.

- Monitor the environment:

  - Observe the effect of display in the nursery; how much do children notice when display is newly presented?; after one day?; after one week?; when the adult has involved them in the presentation?
  - Observe the effects of alteration in the building, e.g. different siting of coat pegs.

- Monitor the effect of increasing the nursery team. If additional parent helpers are added to the team, observe the effect on children's behaviour and activity.
- Monitor links with and provision for the community. Use information from governors to monitor the following:

  - Provision for parents collecting their children at the end of the session; adequacy of waiting space and space for pushchairs.
  - The parents' room; the amount and type of use during a session.
  - Communication links; how the messages put out by the nursery are received by parents; questioning parents about how help offered in literature and information in newsletters is regarded.
  - Keep a check on parents' responses; check which parents attend parents' meetings to see if the meetings are fulfilling majority needs, and note if alternative methods need to be adopted; check how many parents from ethnic-minority groups attend meetings.
  - Monitor the effects of helping parents to become more informed about their child's education; keep a record of questions asked by parents before and after workshops.
  - Devise a regular system for gaining written information from those parents who are willing to give it; provide a box in the

foyer and devise a simple questionnaire for parents to complete, offering their views on arrangements for the transition into the nursery, on the provision of information and on involvement.
- Keep a visitors' list of all those attending a nursery open day.

ASSESSMENT

According to HMI, 'assessment' 'implies the use of measurement and/or grading based on known criteria'.[12] Although nursery teachers may traditionally 'shy away' from measuring children's performance, they more readily accept that systematic checks need to be built into a nursery programme to ensure that the children are thriving. Katz reminds us that difficulties and setbacks occur during normal development, but these should not be regarded as permanent: 'Rather, these difficulties help us notice those periods when the child's own life or situation, for a wide variety of possible reasons, is out of adjustment with his or her emerging needs.'[13]

Bearing in mind that all behaviour is testable in a certain sense, the Dorset nursery document offers some useful general guidelines:

(1) Appropriate assessment procedures need to be adapted for different areas of development, bearing in mind that part of a child's growth is intangible and difficult to measure.
(2) Assessment of young children will vary according to the situation in which the child is working and the people with whom he is involved. Thus the context needs to be mentioned as part of the assessment.
(3) Any assessment of young children should as far as possible be encompassed within the usual activities of the nursery.[14]

Assessment should be considered an integral part of the teacher's work. It provides the means of deciding what children should receive in their future learning programmes, and also gives some indication of their future progress.

All children should therefore be subject to assessment. In a study of assessment methods and purpose in Dumbartonshire nursery schools, a number of individual child observations revealed that many children were spending up to a quarter of their time in aimless activity.[15] This discovery was a surprise, since the immediate impression was of a nursery setting in which all children were busily occupied. Because of this impression, had the observations been directed at one child only, the finding could have been seen as one indicator of special needs.

Once more we return to the value of an experienced teacher's observations and interpretation of those observations. Because of the complex and interrelated nature of early learning and development, these methods are potent assessment tools. These observations need to be planned, however, and an *aide-mémoire* can help to remind teachers of the various aspects of behaviour they should be aware of. Katz suggests using common-sense headings to highlight aspects of development which should be monitored in all children. Some of these assessment categories, such as 'sleep' and 'eating patterns', will depend on detailed information from parents; in other areas a fuller picture of the child will be realized by parents and teachers pooling information. These include consideration of the child's ability to become interested and involved in different activities, his level of play and his responses to authority.

Katz also says that any useful assessment must depend on observations planned over a period of time.[16] She suggests that a four-year-old child will need a four-week period of observation to pick up the behaviour pattern and judge where there may be cause for concern. She warns that these judgements should be made in the knowledge of common deviant behaviour. There is, for instance, little need for concern if a child's appetite is poor due to his often being totally absorbed in pursuits he considers to be more interesting than eating. Warning of potential difficulty comes only where for no clear reason a child scores badly and consistently under a number of headings.

Although well-planned and sensitive observations show what a child is doing, it requires a different approach to reveal his capabilities. A structured situation needs to be set up in which the child can respond to a given situation. The setting for this should be as familiar as possible, and the child must find the activity enjoyable. (Some studies of activities which have aimed to 'test' children in this way are mentioned on page 62–5.)

There is a limited amount of commercial material available for assessment in nursery education. Where it exists it should be used with discrimination. Maureen Shields, in introducing the NFER assessment material, stresses that 'it is a recognized danger that assessments, instead of producing useful information about children's development and performance, may come to determine what is taught. A central purpose has been to serve the needs of teachers, not to impose external standards on them.'[17]

As shown in the Dumbartonshire nursery, assessments of children may throw up useful information about, and have implications for, the nursery provision. Often, however, as indicated in *The Practical Curriculum*, the findings are not used in this way; thus valuable evidence is lost.[18]

Suggested action

Observation for assessment

- Give the child time to settle into the nursery before attempting to assess his performance.
- Determine the times and activities most appropriate to observe specific skills and behaviour; e.g. note what activities encourage children to converse or to use fine motor skills.
- Having observed where the skill or behaviour is best assessed, aim to observe the child across a range of these activities and over a period of time.
- Use a framework for observation of every child to identify those who are generally under-functioning and those who need specific help in certain areas (see Appendix IV).
- Analyse information from these observations as soon as possible after the event.

Setting up situations for assessment

- Determine where abilities need to be checked individually and where a task can be set for a small group; e.g. individual children's pictures may be checked for hand/eye co-ordination and the response to requests to add specific attributes – this can take place with a number of children painting at one time; physical skills can easily be checked with groups of children playing together.
- Use the materials that children are already playing with for assessment; e.g. use miniature play people for discussion and a means of assessing a child's knowledge of his own family. Never attempt to interrupt absorbed play or you will defeat your purpose.
- Check that understanding is sound by transferring the task to other situations; e.g. if a child can sort buttons according to two attributes, can he use this skill with other sorting materials?
- Be sure that the child understands the task expected of him; you will need to know individual children well to adjust the wording and approach accordingly; e.g. when checking children's recall of a story, a child may be prompted by others in the group.
- Plan a progressive task; start with a task that is easy for all the children in the group, making it progressively more difficult according to the abilities of the child in question.

RECORDS

The purpose of records is to provide evidence of assessment, but teachers also need to be clear about the documentation relating to their own planning. Thus two types of record need to be discussed: 'the individual child's record will reflect the agreed curriculum, and the agreed curriculum will be in the possession of the teacher'.[19]

In a recent survey of 125 education authorities and a further in-depth study of one county and one city, a dramatic increase was found in official record forms in nursery schools and classes. The authors saw this as a response to the climate of accountability. In addition to these local authority forms most schools had their own record systems: 'perhaps the predominance of schools' own systems means it will never be possible to suit everyone with a standard system, unless of course it is bland and only meant to be a partial system in the first place'.[20]

Written records need to be kept:

(1) Because no teacher can be aware of every facet of development without some reference material.
(2) In order for the teacher to refer to the pace of individual development over a period of time.
(3) To provide a reference point for other teachers who will be teaching the child.
(4) As evidence of the child's strengths and weaknesses if there is the need to refer to other agencies, e.g. speech therapists, physiotherapists.
(5) To help the teacher to assess effectiveness of her teaching in matching the capabilities of the children.[21]

Despite these aims, in one local authority document Sylva and Moore found that practices did not always match. Only about half the number of education authorities surveyed admitted to nurseries transferring records to infant schools, and in the second study the city nurseries were generally doubtful that their records were read when they did send them. Both surveys indicated that records were rarely used for sharing concerns with any professional bodies outside the education field. The surveys also revealed that nursery assistants were not usually involved in record-keeping. Local authority written guidelines about record-keeping, where they existed, were unlikely to be available to nursery assistants, and only half the local authorities in the survey offered related in-service training to nursery assistants. This is surely a waste of expertise and not in keeping with the principle of teamwork in the nursery.

Both surveys show that nursery staff are not likely to share children's records with parents; even in the nurseries which are inclined to be more open, few parents actually see records. The authors conclude: 'although records are valued as working documents they are not sufficiently used for communication'.[22] With the heightened awareness of the need to work closely with other agencies, particularly in relation to children with special needs, together with the move toward achieving a partnership with parents, attempts will have to be made to use records more meaningfully with both groups.

The form of records in all phases of education must be the result of team agreement. The Schools Council project found that 'Satisfaction with and systematic, even enthusiastic, use of record-keeping systems seems to be guaranteed only in those schools which had produced a record system as a collaborative exercise involving all staff.'[23] Such an exercise should take into consideration the fact that the same records are not needed for all children. A broad check on development, using an instrument such as the observation assessment schedule in Appendix IV, together with progressively graded tasks, needs to be used with every child; any deviation from the norm then identified should be followed and noted in detail. Bearing in mind that children's development and progress are uneven and erratic, individual records are likely to vary tremendously between children and over a period of time for many children.

By consulting children's records, the nursery teacher gains important information about her practice. Patrick Whittaker suggests that 'a school's record system is essentially a device to monitor the curriculum, although frequently it is regarded as a means of ensuring children's progress'.[24] The teacher needs to keep her own records regarding the content, skills, concepts and attitudes that she plans to offer her children. This is the forecast of her intentions and it is meaningful only when matched with a review or record of what was actually received. However experienced the teacher, she still needs to work within this framework. Her records help her to determine the materials or resources needed and to indicate on occasion her method or approach with any particular child. The records should be drawn up jointly with the nursery assistant and other members of the nursery team, and the plans should indicate achievable developmental targets for children.

These documents will also help the teacher refresh her memory as to how the team achieved certain objectives and conversely why an approach failed. The teacher's planning records are important but should be simple and easily kept. The key test for any nursery's recording system is to judge if it offers the required information about matching curriculum to needs.

Suggested action

Decide as a team the format for recording children's progress

- Consider as a staff what information you need in addition to that required in the local authority record.
- Discuss the most effective ways of gathering that information (see 'Assessment', page 134) and the most appropriate way of recording – e.g. a checklist or dialogue on individual children's development. Involve infant staff in any discussion on transfer records; e.g. invite reception teachers from schools you feed to come to the nursery for an informal session; encourage them to be frank about any faults they see in the current system and to state what information they require. The aim should be to reach a compromise; satisfactory policies on transfer records develop only when there is shared understanding of the aims and practices of both nursery and infant phases.

Consider different types of record

No single form of record is appropriate for all types of information. The following formats are all useful for some children some of the time.

- A parental profile of the child when he enters the nursery. This is a useful starting-point, and the teacher can annotate information during the early weeks at school.
- Individual child studies focusing on particular aspects of behaviour and progress over a period of time.
- Completed checklists which may have been used as a curricular *aide-mémoire* for the teacher.
- Transfer records, briefly indicating the individual experiences and achievements of each child.
- Selected examples of children's work, dated and kept over a period of time; these give evidence of progression and are useful for enabling continuity of provision for learning at the next stage of schooling. In certain cases it may be helpful to attach teacher comments to this work indicating how the child set about the task and his general work attitude.

Use records as transfer documents

- Make sure that the material is readable; check that the information is clearly set out, with key points highlighted.
- Check that the records really do communicate required information and ask for a regular review with infant staff.
- Clearly explain to infant staff the criteria used for obtaining the information; they should see any observation schedules used, and procedures and ratings for checking progress should be explained.
- Ensure that information goes to the infant school at an opportune time; e.g. preferably at the end of term preceding the transfer.
- Indicate on records where it would be useful to supplement the written information by meeting and talking with the teacher.

Share records with parents

In many nurseries information is shared informally and regularly with parents. Despite this, consider the benefits of arranging a formal occasion at which it should be possible for all parents to receive information.

- Have a termly occasion entitled 'How Is Your Child Getting On?' Hold this over a period of two days and evenings, using written information on notice-boards, individual letters and a personal approach. Aim for every parent to have an agreed time slot (not less than half an hour). Where parents cannot bring partners, encourage them to bring a friend or translator.

  On this occasion have available the child's personal details; a record of any observations made, with an example of schedules used; results of checks made on progress; and clearly dated samples of children's work including paintings and two- and three-dimensional models.

  The occasion should be used to update any personal details, to inform parents about the nursery view of the child's development and progress and how this view has been gained, and to enable the parent to share concerns and offer views. The interview should end on a positive note, giving a clear indication of future action intended with the child in the nursery and agreed support to be offered at home. Keep notes of this interview.
- In certain areas a written report giving some of this information would be welcomed. However, this should not take the place of an interview; the record can be handed over at consultation, having

formed the basis of discussion or having been taken on a home visit.

Develop a file of personal teacher documents

- Work as a team to determine the main long-term aims you have for the children over the next half-term.
- Using this long-term planning as a framework, keep a daily record of your activity (see Appendix II).
- Share these records with your nursery assistant and allocate groups of children and activities after joint discussion. Check each other's observations and evaluations from time to time to benefit from team judgement.
- Keep examples of children's work and notes indicating the outcomes of approaches and materials used. Within the limits of space, develop an archive of this work for future reference and as a particular resource for students and new practitioners.

EVALUATION

Having gathered information about specific aspects of practice, the teacher can use this to make judgements about current effectiveness. More than that, if this information is to help towards professional growth it needs to inform decisions being made about subsequent action. The evaluation is thus formative rather than just an end in itself.

The Open University evaluation pack suggests six useful questions which any teacher can ask herself and gain insights into her work:

(1) What did the pupils actually do?
(2) What were they learning?
(3) How worthwhile was it?
(4) What did I do?
(5) What did I learn?
(6) What do I intend to do now?[25]

For our purposes the answers to some of the questions should be available through the monitoring, review and assessment procedures described. The answers to questions (3), (5) and (6) should be tackled at this stage.

As mentioned earlier, good teachers have always been self-critical. They can be helped in this by encouragement to reflect on their practice in a systematic way, to share these reflections with colleagues and to work as a team toward a cyclical policy of information gathering, assessment and recording of outcomes, which determines what happens next. Bernard Spodek summarizes this approach: 'Ultimately the evaluation of early childhood educational evaluation must rest on the degree to which we can help to improve the education of all children by what we come to know about the education of some children.'[26] In a nursery where action is determined in this way, all staff should be refining their skills (the more closely you look at something, the more information you are likely to gain), growing in confidence and becoming better able to withstand uninformed criticism and the whims of society. With this professional strength, any external evaluation from the local authority or HMI should be welcomed. The information offered by these bodies will be a useful comparison with the nursery's own judgements.

Teachers of young children, then, need to be seen not only doing good things (this has always tacitly been accepted) but rigorously reviewing their work and acting on this in a way that characterizes the highest-quality practice in any phase of education. HMI suggest that before schools undertake evaluation they need to have achieved a state of readiness.[27] We shall discuss how that state is reached in Chapter 6.

Suggested action

Be realistic

You will achieve effective evaluation only by focusing on one aspect of work at a time.

- If you are fairly new to evaluation, start with a small-scale study; e.g. what happens to (identify target group of children) when they are playing outside? How does (individual child) use his time during the later part of the nursery session? Using this information, measure the effectiveness of your planned programme and judge how it could be improved.
- When you are confident in tackling these studies, work with your nursery assistant and other members of the team on joint ventures.

Act on evaluations

- If the implications for action are wide-ranging, they should be broken down into manageable targets, which in turn should be reviewed; e.g. evaluation confirms that children are spending little time in the art area and the quality of their work is poor –

implications for action: to improve quality of materials used, to change the position of the art area, to make it possible for children to be more self-sufficient in that area, to have more teacher input.

- Try not to embark on a further evaluation until some improvement has been seen in the current area of study.

Communicate your approach to parents and governors

- Where appropriate, hold an informal meeting with parents along the lines of 'How our Practice Is Improved for your Children'. Many parents will be interested and impressed to realize how closely you regard the daily aspect of work.
- Regularly report the processes and outcomes of evaluation to your governors and involve them wherever possible; e.g. seek their views when resiting the art area.

Make full use of external evaluation

This can come about as a result of a brief visit from a nursery colleague in a neighbouring school or a lengthy school inspection. In all cases you should welcome comment or constructive criticism but expect evidence to support any statements made. Weigh these statements against knowledge of your own practice; aim to look more closely at the aspects of practice highlighted.

Take every opportunity to look at your practice with fresh eyes.

REFERENCES

1 Department of Education and Science (DES), *Teaching Quality*, HMSO, London, 1983.
2 DES, *Better Schools: A Summary*, DES publications dispatch centre, 1985.
3 DES, *The School Curriculum* (Circular 6/81, Welsh Office Circular 44/81), DES, London, 1981. DES, *The School Curriculum* (Circular 8/83, Welsh Office Circular 59/83), DES, London, 1983.
4 B. W. Kay, 'The Assessment of Performance Unit: its task and rationale', *Education 3–13*, Vol. 4, No. 2, pp. 108–112.
5 DES, *Quality in Schools: Evaluation and Appraisal*, HMSO, London, 1985.
6 Schools Council, *Guidelines for Internal Review and Development in Schools*, Longman, London, 1984.
7 DES, op. cit. (note 5).
8 Schools Council, *The Practical Curriculum* (Working Paper 70), Methuen, London, 1981.
9 Open University INSET, *Curriculum in Action*, Open University Press, Milton Keynes, 1981.

10 J. Ruddock, 'Teachers in partnership', *Journal of National Association of Inspectors and Educational Advisers*, Spring 1982.
11 DES, op. cit. (note 5).
12 Ibid.
13 L. G. Katz, *More Talks with Teachers*, ERIC Clearinghouse on Elementary and Early Childhood, Urbana, Ill., 1984.
14 Dorset County Council, *The Youngest Children in School*, Dorchester, 1982.
15 M. M. Clark and W. N. Cheyne, *Studies in Pre-School Education*, Hodder & Stoughton, London, 1979.
16 Katz, op. cit. (note 13).
17 M. Bate and M. Smith, *Manual for Assessment in Nursery Education*, National Foundation for Educational Research, Slough, 1978.
18 Schools Council, op. cit. (note 8).
19 M. Dowling and D. E. Dauncey, *Teaching 3–9 Year Olds*, Ward Lock, London, 1984.
20 K. Sylva and E. Moore, 'Record keeping in nurseries', unpublished ms., 1984.
21 Dorset County Council, op. cit. (note 14).
22 Sylva and Moore, op. cit. (note 20).
23 P. Whittaker, *The Primary Head*, Heinemann, London, 1983.
24 Ibid.
25 Open University, op. cit. (note 9).
26 B. Spodek, 'Early childhood education: an overview', *Studies in Educational Evaluation*, Vol. 1.8, No. 3, 1982, p. 24.
27 DES, op. cit. (note 5).

6

THE PROFESSIONAL DEVELOPMENT OF STAFF

Work can be one way of achieving what Herzberg describes as 'that unique human characteristic, the ability to achieve and through achievement to experience psychological growth. The stimuli for the growth needs are tasks that induce growth.'[1] Teaching young children is demanding and yet offers many opportunities for psychological growth. Nursery teachers who seize chances to develop in their work are the ones who have job satisfaction and offer the best of themselves to the children and parents.

In this book we have already dealt with many aspects of professional development. Wherever teachers are thinking about the curriculum or forms of organization they are considering whether they can improve on current practice. This type of development has always been present among teachers but previously happened in an individual and *ad hoc* manner. The accent today is on looking at teacher development in a more thorough and systematic way. One reason for this emphasis is linked with the recognition of the rapidly changing nature of society. There is a need to help teachers respond to this change by providing a dynamic and helpful framework of professional support.

Central government's increasing interest and influence in education have included the whole remit of training and development of staff. The range of HMI surveys both national and in individual schools stresses the need for more sharply focused in-service development, to rectify weaknesses in the service. Present government policies in education are concerned with getting value from its teaching force. The establishment of the Council for the Accreditation of Teacher Education (CATE) to advise the Secretaries of State on approval of initial teacher training courses has meant a rigorous look at the starting-point of the work. Recognizing that local authority funds for in-service development were not always used in the most effective way, central government now allocates money for this purpose. In so far as this has meant that every school and college has had to consider its present and future in-service needs and submit these to be reflected in a local authority bid, the move is a good one.

These developments apply across all phases of education. For nursery teachers there are added reasons for looking to professional support. The focus on nursery curriculum and pedagogy during the past twenty years has led to a much higher profile for the teacher, who is now seen as a central resource for the child's learning rather than as just a benevolent provider. Increasing information about child development and learning, together with stress on the need to engage parents in this process, makes the job potentially more demanding in every way. Moreover, all children under five share similar needs, and yet, as we have seen, there are different forms of educational provision for them. Accommodation for these young children is a good political platform, and some local education authorities have allowed four-year-olds into school with little consideration for their needs or the training requirements of the adults who are to care for and educate them. If these children are to remain in the system it is essential that teachers receive some professional help to tackle the job.

In all, the climate is very conducive to teachers receiving support in their work. The quality of this work depends on the quality of the person and the way they are prepared to do the job. For this reason we touch on initial teacher training as well as the whole range of approaches that may be used to develop staff in post. The concept of the nursery team must also draw attention to the training and support for nursery assistants and other adults working in the nursery. Although courses are mentioned, the accent is on school-based and school-focused development; a dynamic nursery is the best possible seed-bed for professional growth.

SELECTION AND INITIAL TRAINING OF PAID NURSERY STAFF

The initial task facing any training institution is how to determine teaching potential and so be able to select the most appropriate candidates for entry. In recent years academic requirements have increased for all teaching posts in making O-level mathematics compulsory; the more prestigious institutions are now able to recruit from candidates with two and three A-levels. Apart from this, however, the selection of students has developed on an *ad hoc* basis according to different pressures placed on the colleges.

Because personal qualities are so important for teaching, education authority advisers and inspectors have argued that selection procedures for primary teachers should be as much concerned with a candidate's general potential for teaching as with her academic qualifications. According to guidelines produced by the National Association of Inspectors and Educational Advisers (NAIEA) teaching candidates should

(a) relate positively to and lead and enthuse groups of children and also groups of their peers;
(b) adapt pragmatic, empirical and practical approaches to problem solving;
(c) use other media in addition to words in communicating thoughts and feelings;
(d) tolerate a feeling of professional inadequacy in the confidence that they can learn to become proficient.[2]

It is difficult to see how these qualities can be adequately detected by means of the traditional interview and standard reference from a secondary school.

One interesting procedure used to select students for a four-year CNAA-validated B.Ed. course was undertaken at Moray House College of Education. Seventy teaching candidates were each seen for one full day havng been previously informed of the programme for selection. They were required to undertake written responses on personal qualities, intellectual and attitudinal tasks; to take part in leaderless discussion groups and a specially devised simulated teaching task; and to have a traditional interview. The authority had previously been involved in planning the submission for the degree, and the selection panel for these students included advisers, headteachers and teachers, as well as college staff.[3]

This programme was a good attempt to go beyond the usual academic and medical criteria for selection and to look carefully at the personal and interpersonal qualities required for teaching. A long-term study is required to determine the quality of students selected, but two immediate points were highlighted: (1) that such a one-day selection programme, although expensive, is feasible in terms of time; and (2) an anticipated problem, as the programme becomes more established, is that once the selection tasks become known to students their value is lost.

There remains a need for further selection schemes to be carefully monitored over a period of time. Although there is general acceptance that the nursery teacher's work is specialized, there appears to have been no rigorous attempt to consider the role in depth, to analyse the qualities and skills required or to focus on how potential can be determined at point of entry to the college.

Teachers themselves can often recognize potential in future colleagues.

Accordingly, the Council for the Accreditation of Teacher Education (CATE) recommended that experienced teachers should be involved in the selection of teaching students. This recommendation is one of a number which reflect the move to link schools and training institutes more closely (see page 148). CATE was appointed in 1984 as a single council; its terms of reference are 'to advise the Secretaries of State for Education and Science and for Wales on the approval of initial teacher training courses in England and Wales'.[4]

The two approved routes to teacher training remain the four-year B.Ed. or a one-year Postgraduate Certificate of Education, open to graduates. Most colleges offer a nursery training within an Early Childhood Education Phase 3–8. This allows the student to consider the continuity of learning and is also helpful in terms of future career development (see page 170).

CATE's task had presumably involved a consideration of good practice with a view to how the student can be helped to develop this practice. The White Paper on *Teaching Quality* gave only a broad definition in suggesting that a satisfactory teacher needed suitable personal qualities, appropriate academic standards and sufficient professional and practical knowledge and skills.[5] There is no clear requirement coming from teachers themselves. In an analysis of simulated references written by seventy deputy headteachers, Cowan teased out from a list of twenty statements the basis for selecting a good Scale 2 primary teacher. Statements varied enormously, but punctuality and dress were deemed important. Cowan concludes: 'the danger inherent in such a diversity of views is that, if the profession itself is unable to define criteria, outside bodies may be tempted to do so'.[6]

Inspectors and advisers have echoed the need for a model set of aims to be agreed nationally. They suggest that these aims should be based on certain expectations of teachers at the end of their initial training, comprising the awareness of children as individuals, sound classroom management, an understanding of curriculum issues including self-evaluation, and an awareness of the teacher's role within the community and the school.[7]

Since then the CATE recommendations have reflected this last recommendation. The CATE view that courses should pay greater attention to broader aspects of a teacher's work, such as the importance of working with parents and staff collaboration, is to be applauded. New teachers find it particularly difficult to subject their autonomy and the privacy of their classroom to a collaborative approach.[8] They must be helped to see the requirements of working in a corporate way, sometimes opting for compromise so that both adults and children derive benefits from shared skills.

The CATE recommendations should encourage simulated and real experiences for students in team teaching, including ways of working with nursery assistants.

The CATE also recommends that teacher trainers should have had recent success as teachers of the age range to which their training courses are directed. The practical difficulties for colleges arranging this experience are recognized, but the credibility of trainers in the eyes of students and the local education authority (the future employer) is all-important.

A more controversial recommendation is that at least two full years of a four-year B.Ed. course should be given to trainee teachers studying a subject at their own level; only 25 per cent of this two years is allowed to be given to methodology, or the ways of offering subject matter to children. The allocation of time for a one-year postgraduate course is not yet clear.

As far as nursery students are concerned, these CATE recommendations seriously undervalue and restrict opportunities for a programme of child development and pedagogy appropriate to this age range. An understanding of these elements is, however, the very basis of good nursery practice.

Nursery assistants have traditionally been trained by the National Nursery Examination Board (NNEB). More recently the Business and Technical National Diploma in Nursery Nursing provides a two-year training which aims to equip students to work in a variety of settings with young children. Where the NNEB requires entrants to have achieved a good standard of education this is interpreted variously by colleges according to the demands of recruitment. The new diploma course has a more rigid entry requirement of three O-levels or CSE Grade 1 passes, including English and Mathematics.

The Business and Technical diploma course has developed in response to concerns expressed by HMI about the status and opportunities afforded to nursery assistants in the past. The NNEB qualification has offered students no career structure or opportunity to transfer to more advanced courses in higher or further education, while the new diploma is recognized as the equivalent of two A-levels and as an appropriate entry qualification for the B.Ed.

The diploma is at an early stage of development. It currently operates in only three colleges, although a course that offers students a new route into nursery teaching is likely to be well received. The danger is that less flexible entry requirements and accent on the course as preparation for higher education will debar less academic students from training as nursery assistants and from regarding the work as useful and satisfying in its own right.

The NNEB report in 1981 stressed that, rather than lacking in academic rigour, the certificated course offered students an essentially practical training 'as evidence of competence to practise a valuable and particular sort of craft. . . . The essential nature of a craft is that the test of its mastery lies in the practical application of the knowledge, skills and attitudes which have been fostered during a period of apprenticeship and training.'[9] The value of this craft is recognized by all who work with good-quality nursery assistants; but there remains the urgent need for public recognition, reflected through salary increases.

THE NURSERY'S ROLE IN INITIAL TRAINING

The most positive aspects of the CATE are concerned with the relationships to be developed between schools and initial training institutions. Apart from the recommendation that teachers be involved in the selection of students, the DES states that no new initial teacher training course will be approved unless it is supported by a local committee on which there is teacher representation. In addition:

> Institutions, in co-operation with local education authorities and their advisers, should establish links with a number and variety of schools, and courses should be developed and run in close working partnership with those schools. Experienced teachers from schools sharing responsibility with the training institutions for the planning, supervision and support of students' school experience and teaching practice should be given an influential role in the assessment of students' practical performance. They should also be involved in the training of the students within the institutions.[10]

Thus, many nursery teachers, in common with colleagues in other phases of education, will take a central role in determining and supporting the quality of provision for student teachers and their quality of performance.

Practices following these recommendations include the arrangements made for the students' practical training in the nursery, the possibility of nursery teachers being involved as associate tutors in training institutions and their contributions as external examiners or as one of a team of internal assessors appointed to judge student performance. Such a spirit of partnership between training institution and school should help abolish the divide – real or imagined – between ivory towers and chalk faces. Tutors and teachers should become better informed about each other's jobs, and student teachers should have a better opportunity of gaining from shared expertise than ever before.

There are resource implications, however. We have indicated the demanding role of a nursery teacher in school and community. To be useful partners with training institutions, teachers will need to become familiar with the aims, content and approach of initial training courses. They will require time to link with tutors and to have the opportunity for feedback from their sessions.

The quality of a school placement for a student teacher is crucial. Any nursery which is requested to train students should be aware of both the responsibility for offering a model of practice and the need for the student to have the opportunity to practise her skills – with sensitive guidance. This approach means time and planning for the teacher, particularly when working with students during their early period of training. Above all, when taking on these commitments the needs of the children in the nursery and their parents should not suffer in any way.

Local education authorities need to be aware of these implications and decide how they can support practising teachers to train the future teaching population. Both parties should gain from such a partnership, and teachers should consider how tutors and students can enrich work in the nursery.

Similarly there is a need for teachers and nursery assistants to take responsibility for the training of future nursery assistants. This role is more difficult to define, because only a small percentage of students on the course are likely to be employed in education nurseries. However, the training requires all students to have some practical placement with nursery-age children. Even though students may eventually work in varying settings, including hospitals and private houses, there are a number of common learning experiences which can be usefully offered to students by practitioners. These include the practical observation of children, management of children as individuals and in groups and parental relationships with children.

There is a requirement for the Business and Technical National Diploma Validation Council to involve employers of their students in the programme planning. In addition, given a flexible use of resources, there should be scope for teachers and nursery assistants to act as visiting tutors on the course as well as to have close links with course tutors in planning helpful nursery-based training. Both teacher and nursery assistant should share in this training – the former as the team leader. The nursery assistant should be required to have immediate and daily supervision and should also be asked to contribute to the student assessment.

Suggested action

Assistance with student selection

Your contribution should be valued in offering the perspective of the practitioner. Prior to the selection procedures, have in-school discussion on the following:

- What are the main skills required for working with this age group of children?
- What qualities help teachers to be successful with 'difficult' children?
- Discuss the range of skills needed for managing groups of young children.
- What are the most difficult aspects of working with parents? What personal qualities are required for this work?
- What are the qualities of (1) a good team member and (2) a team leader?

These gathered responses may form the criteria for selection. You will then need to discuss how student potential can be identified to meet these criteria.

The teacher as college tutor

Your strength will be your present practical experience with children and your ability to translate theory into practice.

- When taking a session with students, aim to bring the nursery as close to them as possible by slides; a three-dimensional plan of your room with movable furniture; a video of your practice; an arrangement for students to have one session based in your nursery immediately after school.
- Offer examples of your planning and how it develops into practice by giving a plan of one day and following this with slides and examples of children's work, showing some of the day's outcomes.
- Offer different models of monitoring and recording children's progress.
- Offer experiential learning by taking on the role of nursery teacher, with the students as the children, and running through some large-group activity (e.g. story-telling) and a range of small-group work. In time the students can take turns in the role of teacher; the session may be videoed; the student may take some of

the teaching points and be videoed using them with groups of children.

The nursery as a practical training-ground

Opportunities for practical training should include:

- Introductory days in the nursery to consider selected aspects; e.g. the environment for role-play; type, storage and use of large construction toys; the role of the teacher with children who have English as a second language. These limited observations can be written up and discussed with the teacher.
- Blocks of time for a small group of students to work with their tutor on some aspect of nursery practice. The informality and team approach characterizing nursery work make it reasonably easy to accommodate students in this way. The work must be clearly planned with the aim of all parties benefiting from the experience. The focus of study may differ from working on one aspect of development with children to a more complex area involving some classroom research and helpful data being fed back to teachers (see Appendix V).

THE NURSERY TEAM

Whatever the situation she finds herself in, it is most likely that the nursery teacher will be working with other adults at some point during the day. She may be in an open-plan building where she works in a team with other teachers; if she works in a bona-fide nursery she will have a full-time nursery assistant. Even where this full-time assistance is not available, and the teacher is coping with four-year-olds in a primary school, she may have some part-time ancillary help and the assistance of students, and she can choose to invite parents into her classroom to work as volunteer helpers.

All nursery teachers accept the very real difficulties of working alone with a number of young children; teamwork adds another dimension to the job. As leader of such a team the nursery teacher is responsible for the deployment of voluntary and paid staff. She must ensure that they are well briefed and prepared, able to tackle their respective jobs, and that they receive all the necessary feedback to get satisfaction from that work. Unless the teacher takes this responsibility for her team, the nursery is unlikely to reap the full benefit from the shared expertise and energies of these adults. Certain management and interpersonal skills are necessary for the team leader, whatever the size of the team.

The nursery teacher's role is essentially no different from that of any other teacher in that she is an educator. However, because her pupils have very limited experience and undeveloped learning skills she must have particular expertise in child development and the knowledge to plan learning routes for individuals. In a large nursery the teacher may have other teaching colleagues with her. If a team is to function, however, there should be one leader. This may be marked with a post of responsibility, or the leader may be the most experienced teacher. Alternatively, team leadership may be shared, with each teacher taking responsibility for a period of time (less than a term each may mean fragmentation in planning).

The team leader's task is to consult with colleagues, respect their views and use their expertise, taking responsibility for the overall framework in which the children learn. The head of a nursery school is also responsible for policy-making, while a nursery teacher in an attached unit represents the nursery when policy is determined for the whole school.

The nursery assistant has a qualification in the education and care of young children, and her expertise complements that of the teacher. The training for a nursery assistant is shorter, more practically oriented and less academic than teacher training; she is nevertheless qualified to work alongside the teacher and to offer support. This partnership cannot be successful if there is strict role delineation. The nursery assistant has no more been trained to care only for the physical needs of children than the teacher has been to assist only cognitive development. However, the teacher in charge is ultimately responsible for the group of children and, whilst consulting with colleagues, must be ultimately responsible for deciding how the nursery will operate in the best interests of each child. Nursery assistants should be allowed full responsibility for planning part of the programme, but this should always be attuned to the overall structure decided by the teacher. Thus, although the nursery assistant is recognized as the teacher's assistant, the true spirit of the partnership comes through with the assistant working as a full team member.

Parents and members of the community can play a valuable part as volunteer helpers in a nursery. We have considered the usefulness of working with parents in order to offer them a model of handling children and promoting learning. We should also accept that in any community there is a great deal of energy, talent and expertise to be harnessed. Given all that we know about developmental and learning possibilities for young children, the basic staffing ratio is not generous, the recommendation being one teacher and nursery assistant to twenty-five children. The resourceful nursery teacher will therefore look to identify the people who are prepared to offer their time and skills and will plan to use them as additional staff. The nature of this involvement can vary from an occasional contribution to play an instrument, or to help children with woodwork, to a regular commitment to work with a group of children or tackle ancillary jobs in the nursery. Whatever the job, the voluntary helper needs to be prepared beforehand about the children, their needs and the nursery routines.

Where there is a regular commitment, the helper should be clear about the purpose of her work, how it fits into curriculum planning and how she is succeeding. Whilst working in the nursery, the voluntary helper is a member of a team and should be accorded courtesies as such.

Suggested action

Developing a team

- Meet together to share views on teamwork. What are individual expectations of what can be achieved? What are the expectations of a team leader?
- List your own strengths and weaknesses and ask other team members to do the same.
- Aim to work with another team member who will complement your qualities and skills.
- Develop your own clear picture of the strengths and weaknesses in the team by listening to individuals and observing them at work with children and adults.
- Agree working principles as a result of shared experiences; offer the team shared reading; visit another nursery as a group and talk with them about their principles and practices.

Communicating effectively

- Written communication can be displayed and kept updated on attractive notice-boards or in a daily folder. Team members should be asked to scan these papers regularly.
- Important information should be given to the whole team at the same time.
- Each team member should be clear concerning to whom, for whom and for what she is responsible.

- Hold meetings to exchange information and discuss curriculum development. Agree times and dates well in advance and always end the meeting promptly. Never hold a meeting when information can be conveyed just as well in other ways.
- Team planning should occur at the beginning or end of each day to forecast, prepare resources and review the programme and its consequences for children. Arrange some team meetings to include all members of staff; the caretaker, dinner ladies and voluntary helpers each have a contribution to make.

Sharing discussion

- Discuss the children:
  - Select individuals and share information about their development.
  - Select a child known to have a particular strength in one area and share views as to how this can be developed.
  - Agree on expectations for children regarding issues such as tidying up, resolving arguments, levels of noise, personal autonomy and swearing.
  - Share information based on structured observations of children who will require written statements of their needs.
- Discuss the children's products. Consider a range of paintings or models, sharing views on the information they offer about skills and concepts gained.
- Discuss organization. Share views on the pattern of the day; encourage each team member to analyse the strengths and weaknesses of routines.

Working with voluntary helpers

- Recruiting expertise:
  - Ask new parents if they would be willing to help in the nursery; keep a card index file of their interests and talents and the most convenient times for them to help. Keep this updated by asking parents to inform you of any changes in their circumstances or any new area of interest.
  - Ask parents if they have links with any others in the community who would have particular strengths to offer the nursery.

- Interest potential voluntary helpers by suggesting that they spend a trial day with an established helper in the nursery; have a small exhibition of photographed activities involving voluntary helpers with brief explanations indicating the range of work possible; have a simple leaflet for new parents, setting out the above information; include a contribution from a voluntary helper describing her work in one of the nursery newsletters.

- Preparation of voluntary helpers:
  - Where the contribution is to be for a single occasion only, ask the visitor to call into the nursery one day previously for coffee to see the nursery in action. She will then be a familiar face to the children and will be better informed to judge the timing and approach of her session.
  - Regular helpers need a planned induction by attending a briefing meeting; this occasion should be relaxed, with refreshments, but the aim is for the teacher to make clear to the helper how adults work with children and promote learning. Provide the helper with written information; a series of booklets can include topics on 'Cooking with Young Children', 'Working in the Book Area', 'Conversation with Young Children' and 'Mixing Paints and Glues'; these booklets, which can be referred to at leisure in the home, indicate the value placed on the task of the helper.
  - Hold a series of workshops showing the range of activity in the nursery, how materials are prepared and the potential of some of the apparatus for learning and development.

- Include voluntary helpers in the team:
  - Encourage them to use the staff room and on the first occasion make sure that a member of staff escorts them to coffee.
  - Include them in at least some full team meetings and make sure that their views are sought.
  - Provide specific as well as general opportunities for voluntary helpers to discuss their anxieties or report on success in their work.
  - Show appreciation by having a 'thank-you' party for them at the end of year, by offering them a small gift in appreciation of their work, by including them as guests in the end-of-term staff party or supper.

PROBATIONARY TEACHERS

However satisfactory the period of initial training, the student takes a big jump in entering her first teaching post. Experiencing the world of work full-time requires adjustment in itself, and any new job involves establishing oneself with a new group of people, adapting to new routines and having one's competence tested. Hannam suggests that 'because the new teacher feels herself to be an outsider she will tend to see what goes on in the school in sharp outline. Any faults or failings in the system may be uncompromisingly noted and censured.'[11] Most new teachers share some similar experiences of lack of confidence, initial bewilderment and fatigue during the early days. The new nursery teacher is no exception but finds herself in a particularly challenging and responsible position.

This teacher is faced with a new intake of children who are coming to school for the first time. The children need a gentle and sound transition to school, and their parents need to be assured of this and included in the process. These young children have to be assessed at an early stage without the aid of any previous professional records, and the teacher has to keep in touch with their learning and development at a time when the pace of change is rapid. Some of the children's family needs will require the new teacher to liaise and work with other support agencies from an early stage; it can be daunting for an inexperienced teacher to have to attend a case conference and produce relevant evidence in front of other professionals. The nursery teacher also has to assume an immediate leadership role in working with a nursery assistant – a role that can cause anxiety if the assistant is older and more experienced.

A nursery environment can nevertheless also offer particular support by virtue of its informality and teamwork. Young children are highly motivated clients; parents are generally more interested in their nursery children's development than in later years.

Having ensured rigorous guidelines for approval of initial teacher training and emphasized intentions of having a greater say in in-service funding and organization, central government surprisingly gives no detailed indication of its expectations of support for probationary teachers. *Better Schools* baldly states that 'A newly trained teacher needs structured support and guidance during probation and his early years in the profession.'[12] However, this brief statement at least serves to remind local authorities of their responsibilities to new teachers. In 1972 these responsibilities were seriously considered; the White Paper supporting the James Report[13] recommended a lightened teaching load for new teachers and the appointment of professional tutors, who would be directly responsible for the professional development of the new member of staff. These recommendations were made during a time of rapid teacher expansion and in a buoyant financial climate. Since then few authorities have carried out substantial plans for supporting their new teachers, although where professional tutors have been established their work has been well received.

Today there are fewer teachers being trained and a serious current shortage of nursery teachers. It is essential that new nursery teachers are given the maximum support and the best help in becoming first-class practitioners. With so few experienced nursery teachers available, probationary practitioners are in great demand, and schools understandably wanting appropriately trained people are sometimes forced to place a new teacher in difficult circumstances. New nursery teachers can be particularly vulnerable if working in a class attached to a primary school whose headteacher and staff are unaware of the needs of the youngest children in terms of content and approach. There is further concern for the new teacher required to take a large class of young four-year-olds and, despite her training and professional convictions, expected to treat them as infants.

Headteachers and ultimately local education authorities are responsible for their probationary teachers. They should make it possible for the teachers to give of their best to the children. This will involve offering moral support, showing expertise and helping the teacher to benefit from the fund of experience already offered in the nursery, whilst respecting the probationer's need to adopt her own teaching style with the children.

An earlier study has suggested that attitudes of student teachers and new teachers generally remain constant.[14] Attitudes held when starting to teach remain resistant to change, and what change there is tends to diminish during the first year of teaching. However, Hogben and Lawson emphasize that the changes which do occur during the first year depend very much on the school and the way the teacher is accepted as a colleague.[15]

Schools can benefit greatly from the addition of a new teacher. They should remember that supporting a probationer requires time and patience, and that, from the viewpoint of established staff, a motivated young teacher with current expertise can cause disequilibrium.

Suggested action

Provide information before the new teacher takes up post

- The first visit after appointment should be informal, with an opportunity to get to know the building and the staff and get the 'feel' of the school. In turn the staff should be able to see how the new teacher will fit in as a colleague.

- A teacher 'mentor' should be appointed who will be the probationer's first point of contact. Her task is to see that the new teacher has all the information and resources necessary for the job.
- Provide a range of documents to give to the teacher on her first visit. Encourage her to take these away and read them at leisure, noting points for future clarification or discussion. The following documents will be useful: a job description; a staff handbook giving details of school policies and daily routines; a parents' handbook; a list of school dates for the year; a plan of the school and classroom with a list of equipment; a list of children due to start school, with dates of birth and any records or information gained of past experiences; professional details regarding the nursery assistant with whom the teacher will be working – including her work experience, particular areas of expertise and professional interest, and how she has previously worked as a member of the team.

Provide the new teacher with a manageable job

If the teacher is to give of her best she must have maximum opportunity to succeed during her first year.

- With a class of four-year-olds in a primary school, the new teacher should have the largest classroom, a reasonable size group (maximum twenty-eight children) and priority call on the ancillary helper if there is no nursery assistant.
- In a nursery, the new teacher should if possible be placed with a sympathetic nursery assistant, even if this means staff reorganization.
- The new teacher should enter a classroom that has been well maintained, with adequate apparatus that is in good condition. She should not be expected to make apparatus immediately to supplement her resources.
- Offer guidelines to the new teacher in coping with the job; e.g. she should not expect to change her display weekly and maintain the quality; she cannot expect to get to know all the children in the first week – planned in-depth observation and assessment over a period of time are necessary; she should not feel guilty if she does not have the same feelings for all the children but she must try to offer them all her maximum skill and care.

Ensure regular dialogue

The new teacher has been used to sharing her professional thinking and practice with others. This is something that should be encouraged and provided for throughout her teaching career.

- The teacher's mentor should meet with her weekly and offer active support. Within the relationship specific questions should be asked and accepted as proper; e.g. 'What children did you observe this week?' 'What information have you gained?' 'How do you propose to change your approach (the curriculum) in the light of this knowledge?' 'How can I help you with this?'
- The new teacher's records should offer the mentor and head-teacher insights into her understanding of the job, her priorities and planning. New teachers often use a lot of time and energy in keeping copious records and will benefit from having a framework for this from the school. It is not sufficient for these records to be handed in and returned with brief written comments. They should be the basis of professional discussion about the teacher's approach to her work.

Provide a variety of support

- Help the new teacher look at children in depth; share other teachers' observations and comments about children with her; suggest the most appropriate times when she should observe children, e.g. when alone, in a group or talking with an adult.
- Prepare the new teacher for particular aspects of her job; take her to observe a case conference on a child before she is required to contribute; ask her to manage the domestic detail for a parents' workshop so that she can observe the approach used.
- Give her the opportunity to see a range of practice; if she is working alone in a nursery, allow the new teacher to visit to see other models of practice. These visits should be planned and followed through (see page 174–5).
- Help to rectify weaknesses; e.g. relationships – no sound nursery teacher should find this a great problem, but inexperience and anxiety may cause an abrupt or defensive manner. Encourage the new teacher to observe models of counselling and dialogue with parents, which can then be discussed afterwards, helping her to see reasons for the approach.

Respect the new teacher as a valuable colleague

If the teacher is professionally sound and has received a good initial training she should immediately be able to contribute to a nursery. Her self-esteem will be raised if this is openly acknowledged.

- After one term of settling in, give the new teacher an area of responsibility, however small; e.g. checking the parents' notice-board, keeping it in good order and ensuring that relevant and up-to-date information is available; or checking the storage and condition of all sand-play equipment in the nursery. Ask the teacher to report anything noteworthy relating to her responsibility and make any recommendations at staff meetings.
- Take advantage of the new teacher's 'fresh view'; ask her to write a brief report on how she sees the nursery during her first few weeks of work. It should be stressed that the work is for her own use and can be compared with a similar report that she writes at the end of the year. This work should help the teacher appreciate her own development and increased understanding during her first year. In a good trusting staff atmosphere, however, she can be asked to share her material.

EXPANDING HORIZONS

The new teacher is very much concerned with the 'hows' of the work. She needs to feel that she is coping with the children and contributing as a member of staff before she can look further ahead to her development. But when this further stage is reached, the nursery teacher needs to consider her professional needs carefully, preferably in consultation with her head-teacher and in collaboration with the rest of the staff.

In the past, local education authorities largely determined teachers' professional needs and met them through a range of *ad hoc* short courses often held after school and thus available for those practitioners who were keen to take advantage of them. Today the new in-service funding arrangements place considerable responsibility on the schools to determine their own priorities and to do so within a framework of planned development. Thus the teacher's needs must be seen within this framework; there must be space for individual opportunity, but the cost of any one teacher's professional gains will be maximized if they fit into a coherent plan for the nursery.

The grant should when allocated make it possible for schools to request supply cover to allow teachers to be released during school time, as well as funding a range of expertise to help to meet agreed needs. Although the aim of these funding arrangements is basically sound, in ensuring that there is grass-roots-level forward planning, the resources available are insufficient in many cases, and there is a fundamental concern for the nursery section. At the time of writing the DES has made it clear that it does not consider early childhood education to be a national priority for funding. With very few exceptions the priorities attracting higher levels of grant aid are for secondary and further education teachers. There is a danger that local authorities will be attracted to bidding only for those higher grants, leaving early childhood education without the funds to support its work. It is in any case deplorable that nursery assistants, already grossly underpaid for the work they do, are not to have their in-service funded by central government. Let us hope that nursery teachers will be among those fighting for resources to support all members of their team and for a just share of in-service funds, which should be the result of the government acknowledging the significance of a sound start to education.

Not all in-service developments need be costly to be effective, however, and there have been many past examples of expensive initiatives achieving little long-term benefit for teachers and children. We now look at the range of in-service needs that nursery teachers have to help them in their work.

Identification of professional needs

An in-service discussion paper sent to all schools in 1978 suggested that INSET needs should be considered for individual teachers, for groups of staff (the nursery assistants in a large nursery school, or nursery and reception staff in a large primary school) and for the school as a whole.[16]

It is extremely difficult for a practitioner who has been working in a particular way for years and is professionally isolated to be clear about her effectiveness. Before self-evaluation can take place this teacher needs to match her practice against alternative models and look carefully at her abilities. (Many practitioners are tempted to develop those professional areas where they are already strong rather than to address their weaknesses.) Some teachers can manage this alone; most need the help of colleagues to see where they stand professionally.

Where a group of teachers share common problems it will be easier to discuss needs in the light of shared experience. Within the group there may be individuals with particular strengths who can help others to see their limitations. It can be easier to decide as a group that a visit to study different practice would be helpful rather than coming to that decision alone.

However perceptive, no teacher can be aware of all the complexities of her work. Teacher appraisal offers teachers the opportunity to gain further insights. Appraisal has unfortunately had a bad press; it has been equated with accountability and seen in conjunction with conditions of pay. The process can in fact be used as a real aid to determining professional needs, recognizing good practices and improving effectiveness. Employees are generally eager to receive honest feedback about their work. The findings of one major study stressed that, where an established appraisal system was working in schools, teachers were willing to discuss the procedure, and there was a welcoming open school atmosphere and an enhanced professionalism shared by staff.[17]

Appraisal can relate to any area of work and can be applied at any level. Thus the nursery teacher can be appraised on her work in the classroom, her work with parents and her leadership skills with staff. She is likely to be appraised by her headteacher, and may in turn appraise her nursery assistant. However, as with the other aspects of evaluation already discussed, the emphasis should be on self-appraisal, with the appraiser serving as a support. Appraisals can be time-consuming for both parties, and it is important to derive maximum benefit from the process. HMI highlight three limitations in the staff appraisals identified in their study. There was an absence of documentation including any records of the appraisal interview, a lack of established criteria on which to base judgements of practice and little evidence of follow-up or return after the appraisal.[18] These points all deserve serious attention to help teachers to be clear about what is expected of them and to achieve it. If practitioners see this process as straightforward, accommodated in the school system and offering them direct professional help, it should be welcomed.

Areas of professional development to consider

Some indication of the range of information available relating to young children learning has been presented in this book. To avoid feeling overwhelmed by the implications, the nursery teacher should look critically at each of the different aspects of her work and see what she requires to be a first-class practitioner. Each area needs to be regarded in turn. Consider how, through your own efforts and with in-service support from the school and the local education authority, you can achieve professional growth. We suggest some of the main areas for consideration.

Child development

A sound knowledge of child development underpins any professional work with children. Roberts and Tamburrini stress that such study should link theoretical issues with practical observation of children: 'The more one knows the theory of child development the less likely one is to fail to notice significant items in children's behaviour.'[19] Any student of child development needs to recognize that these theories are constantly evolving and expanding. The nursery teacher who tackled the subject twenty years ago is in need of a major update.

Curriculum principles and organizational skills

Knowing the sequence of development and learning, the teacher now needs a thorough grasp of how to match the learning opportunities. She requires a grasp of curriculum principles, a professional repertoire of content and activity and a range of methods to offer curriculum, content and activity most effectively to children. The teacher must also take her organizational skills into account to ensure that she is using all available resources to the best effect.

Classroom-based research

The teacher who wants to know how she is succeeding must be sure that her practice is effectively meeting her planned intentions. If she tackles this rigorously using appropriate methods of investigation she is acting as a researcher. Early research studies were mainly by professional researchers who were trying to judge the success of nursery education in global terms. Today, in the knowledge that many different forms of nursery education exist, the focus is on examining strands of practice in turn to see the effects on children, and helping teachers to develop the techniques to do this: 'The aim in teacher research is for the teacher to attain the eyes of the artist, for it is art that teaches the sensitivity of being attentive to significances that normally remain uncelebrated.'[20]

Nursery practitioners have a particularly strong need to develop these techniques for the following reasons. In work that is so packed with activity there is need to stand back and take stock of what is actually happening. The nursery phase is rich in areas of potential enquiry, but there is little evidence yet of teachers contributing to research, although they need this both to enhance their own professionalism and to help inform policy. Because so much of the young child's learning is private, we need to look at his responses in depth to see how teaching and learning are achieved. Research with young children can be very productive, because the children are so unselfconscious, and the presence of an observer is not likely to inhibit their behaviour or responses.

Openness to change

It may be that such classroom study leads to planning and implementing change. The teacher needs to feel confident with this process herself as well as competent in helping colleagues to change their practice.

Personal relationships

A strong thread running through all aspects of nursery work is the teacher's relationships with children, parents, governors and colleagues. Qualities of warmth, humour and empathy, coupled with a real interest in people and an ability to listen, are, we hope, identified in those successful applicants training for teaching. Such qualities are not easy to teach, and their essential nature becomes apparent only when they are seen to be absent in an otherwise competent teacher.

Awareness of educational issues

In today's educational climate no teacher can afford to be insular. A knowledge of what other agencies provide for young children, as well as the aims and approaches of local infant schools, is important. More than that, an extended professional teacher in any phase will be interested in broad educational issues. The last requirement may seem daunting, bearing in mind the heavy work-load of a nursery teacher, but breadth of vision is helpful in putting one's own work in perspective. The informed, clear-thinking and articulate practitioner is the one on whom we pin our faith for young children in the future.

Ways of promoting professional development

'Effective in-service will involve a variety of activities and it can be initiated and planned by teachers and schools. The activities themselves may take place in the school or an outside centre and may be provided by teachers and outsiders.'[21] How professional needs are met depends very much on the individual teacher's motivation and ambition as well as on the school's and the education authority's ability to find resources to meet perceived and identified needs. In-service development used to be seen in terms of the course which teachers attended on a voluntary basis after school hours. Today this approach is merely a single strand in a web of initiatives that teachers may find relevant to their personal and professional growth.

In-school development

School-based and -focused in-service development allows staff to identify their own concerns and tailor activity to meet these concerns. Increasingly this form of professional development is seen as being most helpful for teachers. Regular school-based in-service courses lead naturally on to school review and evaluation. The school that has reached this stage is functioning at a good professional level, one that is deemed necessary by HMI.[22]

Keast and Carr consider that a school is ready for a school-based course if there is evidence of some of the following:

(a) staff participation in curriculum and organizational planning;
(b) co-operative approaches to teaching as opposed to teaching in isolation;
(c) regular discussions of educational and pedagogical matters;
(d) a staff-room climate which allows uninhibited discussion;
(e) teachers who have developed the skill of learning from each other and from teachers in other schools;
(f) a staff which has developed a theoretical basis for their methods which they can communicate effectively to the local community.[23]

This stage of readiness is essential for any consideration of change in a school. It is also a result of sound leadership from the headteacher, who is the person to determine if change is desirable, opportune and possible.

Leadership and communication

Any nursery is likely to have a mixed staff of varying personalities with different motives for working and different attitudes, hopes, fears and views of the job. Their competence will also vary. Some schools are effective and others less so; some are dynamic institutions, offering opportunities for children and staff, while others have atrophied. The ILEA *Junior School Report* identified several key factors in the more effective establishments,[24] and a small-scale case study considering how primary schools change their curriculum supported these findings.[25] Some of these factors equally relevant to nurseries include a high quality headteacher, a supportive deputy headteacher and a good staff climate.

It was reported recently that Sir Keith Joseph, in giving evidence to the Commons Select Committee with reference to primary schools, mentioned headteachers as being the nearest thing to a 'magic wand' for a school. This belief in the effect of leadership from the top is reflected in a number of studies and reports, and the author's own advisory experience bears it out.

The headteacher provides a model of commitment and standards for the staff; the direction of policy and practice will reflect her philosophy and how this is communicated in the school. Nursery schools are unlikely to have deputy headteachers, but the assistant teacher should be regarded as a second leader who shares the head's philosophy and approach.

Whether in a small nursery or large primary school, the nursery teacher needs to achieve job satisfaction, as do her other colleagues. Clearly the rewards of contact with young children will contribute to this, but satisfaction also largely depends on management structures within. Derek Waters sees the headteacher's role as enabling his staff 'to produce the work of superior people and this will require more sophisticated forms of leadership. Ways need to be found to develop the teachers into a good team who are committed to the aims of the school and use their collective energies towards reaching them.'[26]

Primary teachers interviewed by Nias were dissatisfied with their job partly because of weak leadership, inefficient administration and poor communication. Nias suggests that 'It may even be that much of the stress reported by the teachers is due to the conflict between their job commitment and the inadequacies of their schools as organizations, rather than to the nature of the job itself.'[27]

Nothing is more likely to cause tension in a school than teachers feeling that they do not have access to information. Even in a small school there are teachers who are uninformed about developments and unclear about what is expected of them. Nursery assistants who do not receive information cannot possibly perceive themselves as full team members.

Communication takes place with or without proper networks. However, if a school relies on a grapevine system it must expect distorted messages, misunderstandings, lack of response and frustration among the staff. The smallest nursery unit should establish sound information networks through updated notice-boards, the availability of the head to all staff, regular well-planned staff meetings and clear job descriptions.

The small, intimate nature of a nursery unit is conducive to staff unity. In an organizational climate where staff are encouraged to be personally responsible and interdependent, having a stake in all decision-making, all adults will grow. They will gather strength from one another and, through group identity and increased confidence, will be more inclined to take risks and innovate.

The resource of extra teacher time is always prized in an establishment with young children. A nursery attached to a primary school may use a supply teacher to release nursery and primary staff to view each other's work.

In the nursery the teacher might need extra time to work with a new member of staff or with her nursery assistant on some specific activity. Alternatively the chance for staff to work together or to observe each other's practices without the responsibility of their class can overcome feelings of professional isolation which may well exist in nursery units. Teachers in Partnership was a small research project which explored how teachers could learn from one another.[28] The project's findings indicated that a trusting relationship between pairs of teachers working together is crucial to any successful developments, and that the practitioners most likely to benefit are those who are interested in increasing their own understanding of their work rather than seeking easy answers.

External courses

No school is capable of meeting all the professional needs of its staff. It may be desirable and economically practical to draw together groups of teachers and nursery assistants to offer specific short courses in particular aspects of their work. The short course can be particularly effective in offering training in specific skills, such as different ways of observing children, and the development of interpersonal skills relating to work with colleagues and parents. The relevance of any external course for daily practice is essential. Jean Ruddock suggests that 'the outside course helps the teacher to consider possibilities for development: school-based work enables teachers to select the most suitable starting-points for action from among these possibilities. Their appropriateness can only be tested, in practice, inside the school.'[29]

Longer part-time courses offer staff the chance of a broader and deeper view of their practice. There should be more opportunities to link theory with practice and in some cases to gain some extrinsic reward in accreditation. Again, relevance is all-important; if a written study is involved it should be linked to an aspect of nursery practice; required professional reading should be current, pertinent and manageable.

The main advantage of the part-time long course is that attendance is local. Family commitments can make long-term non-local residential commitments difficult for nursery teachers, a fact that should be sympathetically considered by local authorities. Moreover, the inclusive cost of one-year full-time secondment is approximately £20,000, so it is not surprising that such secondments are increasingly difficult to obtain. In the past full-time secondments were extensively used for individual personal refreshment; now the seconded teacher is likely on her return to be required to contribute to professional development in the authority. A nursery teacher given this opportunity could be a valuable asset to a group of nurseries in helping with curriculum development or assessment and evaluation practices.

Considering other practices

Teachers are constantly eager to see how other colleagues manage their work. The nursery teacher perhaps has a particular need for this support. In many authorities nursery provision is scarce, and practitioners feel isolated; in others, where large numbers of young children are inadequately provided for, the teacher needs every possible support to prevent her from becoming demoralized by not being able to tackle the job properly.

A visit to another nursery can help the teacher stand back and view how a different group of children are accommodated and catered for. As well as looking at other practice in the education system, awareness of other provisions can broaden vision. Playgroups, day nurseries and nursery centres have particular work constraints, priorities and related practices. The nursery teacher may put her own problems into perspective by visiting a provision that is not purpose-built, in seeing evidence of less generous capitation allowance in the amount of equipment provided and in watching colleagues dealing with overwhelming family needs. The ingenuity and flexibility often born from working in difficult circumstances can also help the teacher to see more possibilities in her own setting. A broader knowledge of available provision for young children should also help the teacher evaluate her own contribution to young children's development and learning.

The most satisfactory arrangement is for a supply teacher to be available for visiting purposes. This is expensive, however, and puts the onus on the teacher to ensure that the maximum benefit is derived from the visit. Jean Ruddock suggests that lack of planning limits the potential of the visits.[30] Teachers can certainly return from a day's visit enriched but remembering few specifics.

A profitable visit can give the teacher 'a lift', but it may not be sufficient to refresh someone who has been in the same post for a long time. Despite the current shortage of nursery teachers, in some areas of the country opportunities to move jobs are rare, and there are often family reasons for not moving from the area. Nursery assistants have no means of promotion in education and can remain in one nursery for the whole of their career. There can be an expressed need to have a different experience, and in this case a temporary one-year exchange of post with a colleague can be helpful. A number of local authorities have set a seal of approval on this arrangement, recognizing that two nurseries and two practitioners can benefit professionally as a result of careful planning, without this costing anything.

Teachers as contributors

In any area there are always outstanding practitioners who demonstrate particular skills and qualities in their work. These people should be acknowledged and used in the spirit of shared learning. It is a professional compliment for practitioners to be invited to contribute to in-service work; more than that, it can be a deliberate strategy of professional development for such people. Practitioners may be used in this way informally as a result of an after-school invitation by a nursery group. Or the local authority may request a more substantial contribution from the teacher. In this case adequate support should be given in terms of training and offering non-contact time to prepare and do the work. Contributor teachers should be aware of the need for new skills in working with adults, including answering questions, chairing discussions and making a presentation.

Career development

Any programme of professional development should support those teachers who aspire to further responsibilities and a greater influence in the education system. With the current shortage of nursery expertise, the best teachers must be encouraged to develop their careers – this must not be left to chance.

The nursery teacher is not favourably placed when it comes to promotion. Three factors appear to influence the lack of opportunities: the small size of nursery and primary schools; some existing discrimination against women gaining senior positions; and observed prejudice regarding the nature of nursery teaching.

The way points were allocated within the Burnham system means that small primary schools have never had as good a range of promotion opportunities to offer as compared with the secondary sector. In nursery and infant schools there is almost total absence of senior teacher or Scale 3 posts, and very few nursery schools are of a size to merit the appointment of a deputy headteacher. With negotiations on the restructuring of teacher appointments current it remains to be seen if small units with younger children will continue to be deprived of the opportunity to appoint senior staff.

Although the nursery work-force is still mainly female, the myth that nursery staff are mainly married women has been somewhat dispelled. Although there is no study specific to nursery staff, the NUT research study on *Promotion and the Woman Teacher* showed that of a sample group of 960 primary and secondary teachers only 8 per cent of the under-30s and just over half of the 31–50 age group are married with children: 'thus at any point in time the "average woman teacher" is as likely as not to be childless'.[31] Approximately two-thirds of the teachers involved in this study had taken a break of about eight years to raise their family before returning to teaching, then spending up to twenty-five years in the job. This group of teachers appears to lose a lot in career terms by spending that time away from the classroom, since it is often difficult for the teacher to regain the status and position that she left. Many Scale 2 teachers have to return on Scale 1 for a time, and it is very unlikely that a headteacher resigning for family reasons would gain a headship on her return.

Admittedly the returning teacher is likely to need some updating and reintroduction to her work, particularly in the current climate of rapid change. However, the NUT study showed that only 10 per cent of teachers in the sample were able to attend such a course, and only three-quarters of that small number found the course helpful.

Married women are increasingly taking advantage of maternity provision and returning to work without breaking their career pattern. Nevertheless, in some cases the decision is difficult to make because of the lack of good-quality full-time care facilities for babies and toddlers in many parts of the country.

Of the 94 nursery teachers in the NUT study, 18 per cent were headteachers, but only 5 per cent of the primary teachers were heads. Women stand a good chance of a nursery headship, but these schools are the smallest units, and few authorities are committed to expanding nursery provision in the form of independent schools.

Where nursery classes are attached to primary schools, the chances are still that there will be a headmaster. If the nursery teacher were to apply for such a headship she would stand little or no chance of being appointed. This statement is based on the author's observations of appointments in a number of authorities, together with expressed attitudes to nursery practice. Because teaching young children is often regarded as less demanding intellectually, less rigorous due to informal methodology and less taxing, particularly if the teacher has a nursery assistant, there are reservations regarding the teacher's competence with older children. Even where this prejudice does not exist, the practicality is that other staff are often not inclined or not suitable to be placed in the nursery temporarily, which automatically restricts the nursery teacher's chance of gaining a range of experience with different age groups, a requirement necessary if she is to compete effectively for a senior post in a primary school.

If we are to have nursery trainers and advisers supporting nursery education in a realistic way, it must be within the total educational context. To do this teachers must have the opportunities of a career structure which allows them increased responsibility and leadership in infant and primary schools. Attitudes must change in schools and among officers and governors; local authorities must play a role and provide development opportunities to enable candidates to progress toward headship. One small study which considered the background of successful headteachers found three common factors in all cases: these heads had all experienced working with excellent headteachers at an early stage of their careers; they were all given high degrees of responsibility and the status to undertake responsibility in their former schools; and they showed themselves to be to the fore of curriculum thinking as young teachers.[32] Thus there are implications for headteachers as models for their staff as well as a requirement for heads and local authority officers to be alerted to talented teachers as leadership potential.

The 'secret garden' of professional development

Teachers grow and develop in complex fashion. By institutionalizing and funding in-service work, central government and local educational authorities are touching only one aspect. Katz suggests that 'teachers may need occasional renewals of courage to enable them to sustain their efforts'.[33] Bearing in mind that teachers, like children, are individuals, some need these renewals more than others and find them in different ways. Headteachers who care for their staff personally and professionally are probably in the strongest position to influence an individual teacher's outlook; but it may be that a pint in the pub with a trusted colleague, a visit to someone else's classroom or the effect of some thought-provoking comments from a new member of staff will be the catalyst for change. Whatever it is, the change must be desired if it is to take root and flourish. If the teacher is supported to succeed, she is likely to want to continue learning.

However committed she is, a nursery teacher has her own life, with its personal joys, hopes, fears and problems. These should not be allowed to dominate her professional work but they will affect it. The teacher should appreciate the need for a fulfilling personal existence to help her to give of her best to children.

Suggested action

Identification of professional needs through appraisal

- Preparing for appraisal:
  - Prior discussion about the process is important to ensure that all staff know what is entailed and what benefits can accrue; it may

be helpful initially to work with those who volunteer to be appraised.

- Be clear about the area of work to be appraised (e.g. work with parents, curriculum leadership, classroom teaching).
- Collect evidence to be used at an appraisal interview; ask the appraisee to consider her own work with the help of an *aide-mémoire*; the appraisee's work may be observed by the appraiser; consider tangible evidence of the effects of past work.

- The appraisal interview (see Appendix VI):
  - Give good notice of the date and time of the interview.
  - Allow time for the interview (roughly one to one and a half hours); make sure that the venue is comfortable and that you are uninterrupted.
  - Open the interview by encouraging the teacher to give her views of work during the past term/year; highlight successes but focus on evidence of weaknesses and steer the discussion toward helping change weaknesses to strengths.
  - The emphasis should be on performance of work rather than personality; but the appraiser should end the interview knowing more about the individual being appraised.
- Action after interview:
  - Practical results of the interview should be clear and realistic; they may include a school visit, change of responsibility, increased apparatus, agreement to alter the daily organization.
  - The effect of these outcomes should be monitored, and improvements in work publicly recognized.
  - Any suggestions from those being appraised of how the process could be improved should be considered and where possible acted upon.

Checking your own professional needs

Ask yourself the following questions. Your honest responses may help indicate your priorities for professional support:

- When did I last read a book/attend a course on child development?
- How familiar am I with the post-Piagetian studies mentioned in this book?
- When did I last experiment with a new curriculum activity?

- How able am I to relate my practices to defined principles if a visitor arrives tomorrow?
- How often do my children get bored and 'out of hand'?
- How do others (including my nursery assistant) rate me as a teacher?
- How difficult do I find working with adults as opposed to working with children?

Developing classroom-based research

- Develop the skills; request input from your institute of higher education; ask for contributions on 'Ways of Gathering Evidence'.
- Share your work – through reports at staff meetings and governors' meetings; through linking with other nurseries and asking the teachers' centre to circulate a termly leaflet on 'Classroom Enquiries in Nurseries'.

Developing as a unit

- Offer leadership to the team; delegate as much as possible to free yourself to be the curriculum leader.
- Communicate clearly:
  - Make sure that communication is two-way by giving people the opportunity and time to respond and inviting and respecting their views.
  - Demonstrate your professional concern for all staff by helping them to have a definite and feasible job in which they can succeed and which has been jointly agreed and documented in a job description.
  - Use the most practical and effective means of keeping people informed, e.g. a daily/weekly folder giving details of changes in organization, visitors arriving and after-school meetings.
- Encourage involvement; each member of staff must feel that they have a stake in the nursery:
  - Regular curriculum meetings should be after school and based on a well-prepared agenda.
  - Persuade each member of staff to share one aspect of their practice with others, e.g. how they work with an individual child, how they manage a music group.
  - Encourage discussions and joint decisions on all major policy; an experienced nursery assistant may have very helpful views on

new admission procedures, and a new teacher will add a fresh viewpoint to existing practices.
- Share reading. Build up a resource of professional books which you may share with other nurseries; encourage staff to bring in and share relevant articles and reports which can be discussed at staff meetings.

- Use outside expertise:
  - Invite local people with relevant expertise to contribute to staff meetings, e.g. family-centre matron, social worker supporting young families, headteacher from neighbouring nursery school.
  - Have occasional joint staff meetings with other nurseries and invite the local adviser or education lecturer to lead a discussion.

Seeing how others work

- Plan a regular and balanced programme of visits for all staff in turn which will support jointly agreed needs.
  - Build up a picture of different local provisions for young children: playgroup, day nursery, family centre, childminder, infant school.
  - Visit your local feeder school as part of a liaison programme.
  - Visit other nurseries that are dealing with similar situations to your own.
  - Visit other nurseries and schools that have a reputation for different practices.
- Prepare for the visit:
  - Identify the venue to visit which will best meet needs. Prior information on strengths and interests of local nurseries will help you to make the most suitable choice, together with advice from the local inspectorate.
  - Timing and length of visit: determine whether the visit is most useful during the working day or after contact hours; e.g. classroom layout may be best considered first without the children present, then seeing it in use later.
  - Identify the staff to visit. Where possible staff should visit an establishment to follow up their own particular concerns and interests; visiting in pairs is more profitable, and change may be encouraged by suggesting that an enthusiastic member of staff accompanies a more reticent colleague.

  - Gather maximum information. Ask other staff what information they would like you to get for them from the visit; carefully note this and follow up.

- Follow up the visit:
  - Arrange to share the experiences of the visit with other staff in one or more of the following ways: report back informally at a full staff meeting; relay the information requested by members of staff prior to the visit; compile a school archive of records of visits made and points noted to use for future reference.
  - Thank the host school; a thank-you card may be sent to the children of the host school; the host staff will appreciate some account of how the visit was followed up by the visitors, including a courtesy copy of any report.
  - Consider possible long-term benefits; one visit may occasionally lead to further links including joint curriculum planning or an extended time in the host school; e.g. a temporary exchange of teaching or nursery assistant posts.

External courses

- Seek advice from previous students on the course to check if it is likely to meet your needs.
- A residential course may be most difficult to attend if you have domestic commitments; but it will prove most profitable in terms of developing contacts with others and allowing you to be single-minded and removed from other responsibilities.
- Avoid the danger of feeling overwhelmed by course input and frustrated at not being able to put everything into practice; aim to change one aspect of your work at a time, making sure that you feel confident with this before going further.

Career development

- Aim through reading, discussion and visits to develop a broad perspective of early childhood education to see the range of jobs that may be open to you in the future.
- Plan career moves to complement past experiences; e.g. different catchment areas of schools, type of building, style of leadership, community involvement.
- Plan your own professional development to turn your weaknesses into strengths.

- Accept every opportunity to take on further responsibility; this always provides a good foundation for future promotion.

Teachers as people

- Ensure at least one lunch hour a week when everyone can sit down together to share a light meal.
- Be sympathetic to personal circumstance; a positive response to a request for time to attend to family needs will usually be paid back generously.
- Encourage staff to share personal interest and skills; interest in these may also be a way in to communicating about professional matters.
- Be generous to yourself; as well as giving to others you need to give yourself (1) time to reflect and enjoy the good things of life, (2) positive recognition of your professional achievements and (3) the opportunity to enjoy and develop in your work.

REFERENCES

1 F. Herzberg, 'One more time – how do you motivate employees?', in L. Davis and J. Taylor (eds.), *Design of Jobs*, Penguin, Harmondsworth, 1972.

2 National Association of Inspectors and Educational Advisers (NAIEA), *The Professional Aspects of Initial Training for Primary School Teachers*, NAIEA Publications, Letchworth, Hants, 1984.

3 J.D. Wilson and L. Mitchell, 'Developing a programme for selecting primary teachers', *Journal of Education for Teaching*, Vol. 11, No. 3, October 1985, pp. 264–280.

4 Department of Education and Science (DES), *Initial Teacher Training: Approval of Courses* (Circular 31/84), DES, London, 1984.

5 DES, *Teaching Quality*, HMSO, London, 1983.

6 G. Cowan, 'What makes a good primary teacher', *Journal of Education for Teaching*, Vol. 10, No. 3, October 1984, pp. 256–258.

7 NAIEA, op. cit. (note 2).

8 E.J. Hatton, 'Team teaching and teacher orientation to work', *Journal of Education for Teaching*, Vol. 11, No. 3. October 1985, p. 228.

9 National Nursery Examination Board (NNEB), *A Future for Nursery Nursing*, NNEB, London, 1981.

10 DES, op. cit. (note 4) (Annex).

11 C. Hannam, P. Smyth and M. Stephenson, *The First Year of Teaching*, Penguin, Harmondsworth, 1976.

12 DES, *Better Schools*, HMSO, London, 1985.

13 DES, *Teacher Education and Training* (James Report), HMSO, London, 1972.

14 D.D. Lortie, *School Teacher: A Sociological Study*, The University of Chicago Press, 1975.
15 D. Hogben and M.S. Lawson, 'Trainee and beginning teacher attitude and change', *Journal of Education for Teaching*, Vol. 10, No. 2, May 1984, pp. 135–53.
16 Induction and In-Service Training Sub-Committee of the Advisory Committee on the Supply and Training of Teachers (INSET Sub-Committee), *Making Inset Work*, DES, London, 1978.
17 Suffolk Education Department, *Those Having Torches . . . Teacher Appraisal: A Study*, Suffolk County Council, Ipswich, 1985.
18 DES, *Quality in Schools: Evaluation and Appraisal*, HMSO, London, 1985.
19 M. Roberts and J. Tamburrini, *Child Development 0–5*, Holmes McDougall, Edinburgh, 1981.
20 J. Ruddock, 'The improvement of the art of teaching through research', *Cambridge Journal of Education*, Vol. 15, No. 3, p. 122.
21 INSET Sub-Committee, op. cit. (note 16).
22 DES, op. cit. (note 18).
23 D. Keast and V. Carr, 'School-based INSET: interim evaluation', *British Journal of In-service Education*, Summer 1979, p. 25.
24 Inner London Education Authority (ILEA), *The Junior School Report*, ILEA Research and Statistics Branch, London, 1986.
25 M. Dowling, 'Curriculum change in primary schools: a case study approach', in Schools Development Curriculum Council, *Link*, Spring 1987.
26 D. Waters, *Management and Headship in the Primary School*, Ward Lock, London, 1979.
27 J. Nias, 'Teacher satisfaction and dissatisfaction: Herzberg's "two-factor" hypothesis revisited', *British Journal of Sociology of Education*, Vol. 2, No. 3, pp. 235–45.
28 J. Ruddock, 'Teachers in partnership', *Journal of NAIEA*, Spring 1982, p. 14.
29 J. Ruddock, *Making the Most of the Short In-Service Courses* (Schools Council Working Paper 71), Methuen, London, 1982.
30 Ruddock, op. cit. (note 28).
31 National Union of Teachers (NUT), *Promotion and the Woman Teacher*, NUT/Equal Opportunities Commission, London, 1980.
32 Dowling, op. cit. (note 25).
33 L.G. Katz, *More Talks with Teachers*, ERIC Clearinghouse on Elementary and Early Childhood, Urbana, Ill., 1984.

APPENDICES

I

SAMPLE HANDOUT FOR NEW PARENTS

Helping your child settle happily in the nursery

Your child will be excited about coming to the nursery, but when he arrives he may find some things difficult.

He may find that mixing with other children is not easy.

He may be worried about using a different lavatory or having to hang up his coat with those of other children.

He may find leaving you difficult.

He may be happy to leave you at first, but then later want you to stay.

What you can do to help

Help your child to understand that he will go to the nursery every day (sometimes children think that the experience ends after day one!).

Even if you are worried about your child settling happily, try to keep these worries to yourself. Make it clear to your child that you are sure he will enjoy himself.

Make it clear to your child that you will stay with him for his first day and when you leave him it will be for only a short time.

If your child is very worried about being left, make sure that you take off your coat to assure him that you are staying.

Explain to your child what you will do in the time that you leave him and later collect him from the nursery. He will be reassured to know that you are shopping for his tea or making his bed.

When you feel it is time to leave your child, tell him, tell your teacher and leave straight away.

Make the first few separations brief and enjoy the company of others, in the parents' room.

Always collect your child in good time – he will be waiting for you.

Be patient. If you stay with your child for some time at first he is less likely to want you to stay later.

What we can do to help

You and your child will have one teacher who will be particularly interested in helping your child to settle happily.

This teacher will watch your child closely during the first few weeks. She will check who he plays with, what his interests are and see if he has any worries.

Your teacher will work with your child so that she can get to know him well and find out his strengths.

What more can we do to help?

Please let us know if you have worries about your child. We want to work closely with you. Help us to help your child.

II

SAMPLE FORECAST AND REVIEW OF PLANNING FOR TEACHER AND NURSERY ASSISTANT

(Keep a supply of these record sheets with duplicated headings for easy use.)

Date: Tuesday, 6 April

Names of children	*Aim*	*Activity/ resources*	*Approach*	*Observations of outcomes*	*Evaluation and implications for action*
Rick Janette Mary Dean Wayne } my group	Check recall skills.	Book area – 'Three Little Pigs'.	Remind children how we enjoyed story yesterday (checked that this was new story for all of them). Suggest that they tell it to me – if difficult use pictures as prompt.	Rick dominated – clearly recalled every detail. Janette, Dean, Mary confident with most details. Wayne only contributed 'pig'.	Rick to tell story to group tomorrow. Repeat story with Wayne.

Charlotte Grant Steve Samantha	Sarah's (NNEB) group	Check sorting by two attributes.	Logi blocks.	Allow free play. Ask children individually and in turn to identify blocks by means of informal game.	Steve and Samantha identified correctly every time.
					Try with buttons tomorrow.
					Grant was muddled and lost interest.
					Try Grant on one to one.
					Charlotte made two mistakes.
					Repeat activity.

III

DETERMINING PRIORITIES FOR REVIEW

Please indicate (by ticking in the appropriate column):

(1) whether you think each aspect in the nursery is an area of strength, weakness, or satisfactory;
(2) whether you feel that these aspects would be desirable to review (i.e. gather further information and consider more closely).

Aspect of the nursery	*Strength*	*Satisfactory*	*Weakness*	*Would benefit from review*	
				Yes	*No*
Curriculum					
Children as individuals					
Matching tasks					
Meeting multi-ethnic needs					
Provision for learning difficulties					
Liaison and continuity					
Transition from home to nursery					
The move to infant school					
Active learning					
Exploration through the senses					
Structured play					
Language development					
Mathematical development					
Spatial awareness					

Aspect of the nursery	*Strength*	*Satisfactory*	*Weakness*	*Would benefit from review*	
				Yes	*No*
Beginnings of measurement					
Beginnings of logic					
Number					
Representing experiences through:					
A broad curriculum					
Symbolic play					
Painting and drawing					
Construction and model-making					
Making sounds					
Dance and movement					
Linking experiences to pictures and written symbols					
Providing a balanced curriculum					
Fostering desirable qualities					
Self-sufficiency					
Sociability					
Moral awareness					
Empathy					
Links with the family					
Initial links with families					
Maintaining communication					
Pastoral support for families					
Making parents aware of their educational role					

Aspect of the nursery	*Strength*	*Satisfactory*	*Weakness*	*Would benefit from review*	
				Yes	*No*
Links with other agencies					
Organization					
Environment					
Furniture and fittings					
Selection and purchase of equipment					
Daily routines					
Teaching and learning					
Educational display					
Assessment and record-keeping					
Professional development of staff					
Conversance with research and current trends					
Updating on materials and methodologies					
Teamwork					
Awareness of other agencies					
Training of students					
Links with community and governors					

Bearing in mind that you may wish to review a strength as well as a weakness please identify your one priority for further consideration during the next term.

IV

SAMPLE OBSERVATION SCHEDULE FOR ASSESSMENT

It is suggested that this schedule is used to observe the child during the latter part of his first term in school, over a period of three weeks to gain a general picture of development.

Child's name: ....

Date observation started: .... Completed: ....

Please circle the number of the statement under each heading which most accurately describes the behaviour of performance observed.

Relationship with peers

(1) Takes a leadership role in a group which includes older children and may invite more reluctant peers to participate.
(2) Joins in most group activity with ease.
(3) Joins in with group activity when invited to do so but this rarely happens.
(4) Shows interest in activity with others but always observes rather than participates.
(5) Clearly prefers his own company: avoids contacts with other children.

Reactions to authority

(1) Occasionally resistant to adult requests, but cheerfully complies with persuasion and responds to reasons given for request.
(2) Resistant to adult authority if absorbed with his own interests.
(3) Reacts strongly against adult authority but will temper his response in the light of the responses from peers.
(4) Strongly resists any implication of adult authority at all times: constantly pushes against boundaries of behaviour.
(5) Submissive attitude – never questions adult authority – appears anxious when adult requests are made.

Self-sufficiency

(1) Attempts new tasks with confidence and enjoys new experiences: makes decisions without reference to adult.
(2) Usually self-sufficient but sometimes needs adult's support with a new activity.
(3) Self-sufficient while there are no problems: in the light of difficulty immediately turns to an adult for help.
(4) Needs an adult nearby and requires regular reassurance to follow a course of action.
(5) Clinging and almost totally dependent on one adult.

Involvement in varied activity

(1) Regularly involved with a full range of activities and combines materials from different activity areas for his own purposes.
(2) Has clear preference for particular activity but will move if new experience or apparatus is on offer.
(3) Has clear preference for particular activity but can be persuaded to move.
(4) Always starts the day in one activity area and is very reluctant to move.
(5) Always stays in one activity area and resists encouragement to move.

Interest and concentration

(1) Regularly takes an active and sustained interest in a task and is oblivious to distractions around.
(2) Willing to complete a task with an eye for detail when interested.
(3) Will complete a task with encouragement and occasional help from adult.
(4) Always wants to try new activities but quickly loses interest and 'flits'.
(5) Has little interest in becoming involved in any activity but hovers on the sidelines.

Use of language

(1) Converses with ease: initiates talk with adults and peers: is capable of explaining his own meaning if it is not clear: projects and hypothesizes.
(2) Takes an equal part in a conversation. With encouragement can explain a process and expand points.

(3) Responds to conversations: occasionally reports on present and past experiences without prompting.
(4) Uses talk mainly to direct his own actions and those of others in play: may bring up a point of interest but is unwilling to do this or listen to others.
(5) Main use to refer to his own physical needs and maintain his interest: responds with single words or brief phrases if approached in conversation.

Personal buoyancy

(1) Constant sunny, resilient disposition – rarely thwarted.
(2) Occasionally upset if thwarted by adult or child – otherwise cheerful.
(3) Often tearful and upset if thwarted but rapidly recovers.
(4) Regularly moody and withdrawn for no apparent reason.
(5) Prone to outbursts of uncontrollable temper tantrum for no apparent reason.

(This sample is a useful starting-point – the schedule will be more valuable for you if the statements are discussed and amended in the light of your needs.)

V

INITIAL TEACHER TRAINING: MODELS FOR SCHOOL-BASED STUDY

Model (1): Observing and modifying children's learning behaviour

Tutor and eight students working in 100-place nursery unit.

Aim: To help students observe behaviour, the effect it has on learning and the teacher's role in helping to change it.

Approach: With the aid of the teacher and tutor the student identifies certain behaviours in children which require modifying; e.g. distractability, dependency, attention-seeking.

Programme for one term – one day a week.

Each student works with one or two children considering background information, observing behaviour and then planning positive strategies to modify the behaviour.

The nursery teacher should keep students briefed about the work tackled with the children during the week.

The students will regularly report on reactions to their planned activities and on any observable changes in their target children. The tutor and teacher will help to analyse this information with the rest of the group.

Model (2): Liaison and continuity of learning

Tutor and eight students working in a 100-place nursery unit and two reception classes, involving two nursery teachers, two nursery assistants and two reception teachers.

Aim: To consider the differences of approach to teaching and learning in nursery and reception classes: to learn about and appreciate the need for some differences and highlight areas where differences could be improved.

Approach: Students in nursery and reception classes to work with small groups of children but to focus on different aspects; e.g. daily routines and expectations of children, choices available to children, environment, use of space and layout of activities, children's use of language with peers and adults.

Programme for one term – one day a week.

Students to work in pairs, each pair to work for half a term in the nursery and half a term in one reception class.

The tutor to consult with the teacher about the groups of children and appropriate activities for the students' involvement: also to link with students throughout their day in school, to plan briefing sessions at the start of the day and follow-up discussions at the end of the day with the teaching staff present.

VI
APPRAISAL INTERVIEW CASE STUDY

You can use this case study in the following ways:

(1) As a topic for general discussion prior to appraisal being introduced for staff.
(2) As a simulation exercise in which case the following instructions apply:
    (a) Within a group of three agree on role of appraiser, appraisee and observer.
    (b) Allow the appraiser to read paper A (characters involved) and paper C (her own character study), the appraisee to read papers A and B and the observer to read all three papers, thus having information about both characters.
    (c) The task is for the appraiser to interview the appraisee while being observed and to achieve the aims as set out on page 172.
    (d) After the interview the characters look at each other's roles and the observer feeds back information on respective performances and views as to how far the aims were met.

Paper A: Characters involved

The appraiser – Avril Simpson: age 30

Previous experience: B.Ed with early-years specialization. Avril gained a Scale 2 post in a nursery class after two years and has been in her present post as Head of Green End Nursery School for only six months. She teaches full time and has Janet as her nursery assistant.

Personal and professional qualities: Hardworking, serious, caring personality who worries about her job. Although sensitive to adult needs Avril does not find communication easy. Her interest and curriculum strength is in early language development where she gained a reputation in her previous school for effective work with children.

The appraisee – Janet Cox: age 31

Previous training and experience: Gained her NNEB qualification after a very successful course at a college with a high reputation for training.

Worked for one year in local day nursery but since then has been in Green End Nursery School where she is the longest-serving nursery assistant.

Personal and professional qualities: Able, outgoing and occasionally impatient. Interest and ability with distractable and 'difficult' children. Particularly skilled with display and generally committed to work.

Paper B

You play the role of Avril Simpson. In so doing you will have to be yourself but bear in mind Avril's situation and particular concerns.

Avril was thrilled to have gained this headship but now she is not so sure that she will make a good leader as her relationship with Janet appears to have broken down.

Avril saw immediately that Janet was talented, particularly with her display, although she felt that children could be more involved in selecting and putting up their work. Anyway, there was a need to tighten up on security: by asking Janet for her school key which she appears to have used to come into school on Sunday afternoons to work on display, Avril feels that she might now have this work integrated more into the curriculum.

Janet also spends a great deal of time with a small group of distractable boys with whom she works well, but she appears to think that she has exclusive responsibility for children with special needs. Avril also knows that these are the very children who will benefit from language experiences that she has devised. She has, therefore, insisted that Janet works within a planned weekly framework which allows Avril daily time to work with this group of children.

Avril is determined to develop regular curriculum staff meetings. The other staff all agree with her that these are best arranged after school but Janet has deliberately avoided the question and made a last-minute excuse not to attend the first meeting held two weeks ago.

Avril admires Janet's easy, confident manner with parents and children and feels very fortunate to have such a talented nursery assistant. However, she worries that Janet does not respect her professionally and that her commitment to work is lessening.

She hopes that the appraisal interview will improve matters and has arranged this during school hours.

Paper C: Character study

You play the role of Janet Cox. In so doing you will have to be yourself but bear in mind Janet's situation and particular concerns.

Janet was initially very pleased to work with her new headteacher but is rapidly becoming disenchanted. In the past Janet was given a free hand in the nursery which she enjoyed although she felt that her work was never really understood. Now she is more restricted and asked to work within a fairly tight framework which is discussed weekly with the headteacher. Janet acknowledges that everyone is much clearer about their respective areas of work but she does not have the same contact with the children with learning difficulties; they are having closer attention from Avril.

Janet is aware of her talents with display and the previous head used to praise her constantly for the lovely work which she would always come into school on a Sunday afternoon to arrange. Avril has not commented on her work and Janet no longer has free access to the school because she has been asked to give up her school key for security purposes. This she resents and sees as a sign of her headteacher's lack of trust in her.

Janet respects Avril and knows that she can learn a great deal from her, particularly in language work; however, she feels undervalued and under-used. Because of this Janet has decided that she will not bother so much about her display and she has refused to attend staff curriculum meetings after school, although in principle she thinks that these are a good idea.

This appraisal idea sounds to be a new gimmick but Janet supposes that she has no choice as Avril has said that the interview can be arranged during school time.

INDEX

AUTHOR INDEX